D1738493

POLITICAL ORGANIZING IN GRASSROOTS POLITICS

Daniel M. Russell
Springfield College

UNIVERSITY
PRESS OF
AMERICA

Lanham • New York • London

University Press of America®, Inc.

4720 Boston Way
Lanham, MD 20706

3 Henrietta Street
London WC2E 8LU England

British Cataloging in Publication Information Available

Library of Congress Cataloging-in-Publication Data

Russell, Daniel M., 1948–   .
Political organizing in grassroots politics / by Daniel M. Russell.
p.   cm.
1. Boston ACORN (Organization).   2. Community
organization—Massachusetts—Boston—Case studies.
3. ACORN (Organization).   4. Community organization—
United States—Case studies.   I. Title.
HN80.B7R87   1989   322.4'4'0973—dc20   89–22757 CIP

ISBN 0–8191–7618–4 (alk. paper)
ISBN 0–8191–7619–2 (pbk. : alk. paper)

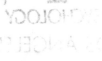

DEDICATION

To Beth With Love

TABLE OF CONTENTS

LIST OF TABLES

PREFACE

This study began with a desire to combine political science research with a contribution to social justice. My initial involvement in political organizing, in 1976, was with a low- and moderate-income community organization. That experience made a lasting impression on me both because of the group's accomplishments and because it whetted my curiosity about low- and moderate-income political organizing. Ten years later, these feelings have contributed to the writing of this study.

Numerous individuals have aided in the successful completion of this effort. The success of my work in 1976 was largely due to the help and cooperation of Wade Rathke, Alice Baudy, and Zach Pollett. These three remarkable individuals were extremely helpful in that effort. Since that time, my continued involvement in ACORN has borne fruit only because of the acceptance and warmth of the members and organizers I encountered in my activities with ACORN and in informal settings.

This study of Boston ACORN was aided on two ends, in Boston and in Amherst. In Boston, I had the privilege to work with Barbra Gross and her staff and the members of Boston ACORN. They were not only informative and insightful, but a pleasure to know. The time I spent in research in Boston was dear to me as a result.

In Amherst, on the academic end of the project, particular thanks are due Jerome Mileur. His careful and patient guidance throughout was essential to the entire project. Debra Gross provided essential substantive input -- complemented by Glen Gordon's profound sense of good scholarship. I also wish to thank the members of my committee: Gordon Sutton, whose insight has been invaluable and John Fenton, whose participation is highly regarded and appreciated. Also essential to the success of this study was Dr. Charles D. Hadley whose professional guidance and friendship have made any of my successes in political science possible.

I also wish to express my appreciation to my parents, who so often provided the material and supportive wherewithal to complete this work. Finally, I owe my wife, Beth, a tremendous debt and wish to thank her for her support throughout -- when things were going smoothly and when they were not.

INTRODUCTION

> Enough is enough. We will wait no longer for the
> crumbs at America's door. We will not be meek,
> but mighty. We will not starve on past promises,
> but feast on future dreams.
>   --ACORN People's Platform[1]

The right to assert dissenting political views in American politics is protected by Constitutional guarantees, but there are no guarantees that efforts to promote those views will succeed. The authors of the statement above, members of the Association of Community Organizations for Reform Now (ACORN), have chosen a particularly difficult goal: empowerment of low- to moderate-income Americans through a national organization of community organizations. ACORN's degree of success is due to a well-considered plan executed by dedicated and talented professionals and volunteers. It has been a privilege to participate in ACORN political activities on a number of occasions.

I became involved in ACORN out of political conviction, but quickly discovered that this group had much to teach about the American political system. My association with ACORN over the last ten years has convinced me that it is a remarkable group of people. My conversations and observations have provided me with numerous insights into politics, communities, and organizations. This is why I chose to study ACORN and use the perceptions of ACORN participants as a primary source of data.

The most recent studies of voluntary political organizations by Terry Moe[2] and David Knoke and James R. Wood[3] use surveys and statistical analysis of survey responses. Norman I. Fainstein and Susan S. Fainstein[4] use interviews and historical data. As yet, there have been no major studies of low-income organizations that used participant-observation.

Each approach has its strengths and weaknesses. Surveys assure a valid sample through a large body of respondents. Moreover, their data can be statistically manipulated to determine relationships among variables. But they do not allow the researcher to probe the respondents' responses to assure a common understanding of terms, or to allow respondents to offer their own ideas of what is important. Finally, as Sidney Verba and Norman Nie's study illustrates, it is also difficult to establish causality.[5]

Interviews provide opportunities to delve into the respondents' minds and explore their ideas. Open-ended questions allow respondents to contribute their own insights and to clarify points that the researcher may not appreciate at the beginning of the study. The number of interviewees must remain small, however; this raises the possibility of an unrepresentative sampling. The data derived from interviews is also vulnerable to potential bias in the interviewing process.

The participant-observation process also allows trained social scientists to report experiences and perceptions. However, this process contains even greater potential for bias than interviewing, because the participant comes to share values and orientations of the group. Thus, each technique offers opportunities and contains pitfalls for the researcher.

Interviews for this study were designed to ascertain how Boston ACORN (as have other ACORN chapters since 1970) has succeeded in attracting and maintaining members since its founding in 1980. Data was collected through open-ended interviews with activists, leaders, and organizers of Boston ACORN.

The interviews probed the following kinds of questions:*

(1) How does the organization attract members and keep them active?

(2) To what extent do members get involved in the organization's activities?

(3) What do the members perceive as the organization's goals?

(4) How much consensus is there on important political issues among members, and between members and organizers?

(5) How are important decisions made in ACORN?

(6) What are the members' perceptions of the means by which ACORN pursues political goals?

---

*See Appendix I for the interview questionnaire.

(7) What are the members' feelings of efficacy and perceptions of politicians?

Responses to these questions yield a picture of the means by which ACORN, a voluntary organization, is able to get its constituents to join and contribute their time, energy, and other resources to the organization on a sustained basis. In addition, it provides insights into the internal politics of the organization and the self-perceived impact of membership on the constituents.

The Interviews

Volunteers for interviews in this study were chosen by asking the Head Organizer of Boston ACORN for a list of willing interviewees. Therefore, the interviewees do not constitute a random sample of ACORN members. Several of the interviewees signed up at a board meeting of the organization; others were contacted by phone by the organizers. The sample is biased in favor of older members and leaders, but includes some who are newer and less active. I also interviewed all of the professional organizers who were then assigned to the Boston office.

The questionnaire was designed to satisfy three criteria: (1) it addresses the basic questions raised in the literature; (2) it is sufficiently open-ended to stimulate independent responses from the interviewees; and (3) it addresses experiences that might result from ACORN activities, e.g., confrontational tactics, neighborhood organizing, and participatory membership.

The interview was administered in a conventional format. At the end of the interview, respondents were asked if there were any topics they felt were not covered adequately by the questionnaire. Several added comments about their experiences. Finally, interviewees were asked to complete a second, demographically oriented questionnaire, the text of which is also in Appendix I.

All interviewees agreed to have the interview taped to insure accuracy. The researcher advised the interviewees that no part of the interview would be attributed to them without their explicit permission, to preserve confidentiality. All interviews with members, except one, took place in private homes; the exception was held in a private room in the ACORN office. The interviews with organizers were conducted in private at the ACORN office or in a deli across the street.

The interviewees were quite generous with their time and ideas. Their data provide many insights into the experiences and perceptions of this dynamic and interesting group of people and contribute to the understanding of voluntary political organizations.

Notes to Introduction

[1]ACORN People's Platform in Program to ACORN 1980 Convention (mimeographed, n.d.).

[2]Terry M. Moe, _The Organization of Interests_ (Chicago: Univ. of Chicago Press, 1980).

[3]David Knoke and James R. Wood, _Organized for Action_ (New Brunswick, NJ: Rutgers Univ. Press, 1981).

[4]Norman I. Fainstein and Susan S. Fainstein, _Urban Political Movements_ (Englewood Cliffs, NJ: Prentice-Hall, Inc., 1974).

[5]Sidney Verba and Norman Nie, _Participation in America_ (New York: Harper and Row, 1972), p. 200.

C H A P T E R   I

THEORIES OF POLITICAL ORGANIZATION

On July 12, 1980, thirteen delegates to the Republican National Convention accepted an invitation to tour Detroit's poorer neighborhoods. It came from the Association of Community Organizations for Reform Now (ACORN), a leftist organization that represents low- and moderate-income people.

ACORN was trying to point out the contrast between the tremendous development in Detroit's Renaissance Center and other neighborhoods which had not benefitted from federal development grants. ACORN members rode with the delegates on a church bus. During the ride, they offered their solutions to the problems of urban decay in a document they called "ACORN's People's Platform." Their suggestions included federal public housing, low- and moderate-income representation on corporate boards, and bank financing for rehabilitation of low-income housing.[1] According to New York Times reporter Iver Peterson, one delegate, a Ms. Joanne Mueller, of Hibbing, Minnesota, made an interesting comment: "I tried to tell them if they had a concern they should get involved in politics, that's what I did."[2]

Despite her willingness to participate in ACORN's tour of Detroit and her concern that social problems be addressed through political action and membership in political organizations, Ms. Mueller failed to recognize political activity when it confronted her. Moreover, she failed to recognize a relatively sophisticated form of political activity, undertaken by people from the lower end of the income scale who generally do not participate in American politics. Indeed, it is striking that low- and moderate-income people participated at all in this media event, interacting with the more conservative of the two major parties while it was nominating Ronald Reagan, its most conservative candidate in almost twenty years.

Political scientists have not taken such activities for granted or failed to recognize their scarcity among low-income Americans. Rather, they have attempted to develop theories to explain when and how such activities are likely to occur. While much of this thinking focuses on middle- and upper-income

1

Americans, the long commitment of the American left to organizing and mobilizing lower income people has shed some light on that phenomenon as well. This study attempts to clarify certain issues in the general literature on political organizing by applying them in a case study of ACORN. I will test organizational theories against ACORN's efforts to organize low- and moderate-income people for sustained political action, beginning with a review of basic concepts in the literature.

Theories of Political Organization

It is precisely the kind of activity in which ACORN engages -- overt attempts to influence public policy -- that provides the impetus for the study of political organizations in American political science. Arthur F. Bentley, writing in 1908, attempted to develop a systematic understanding of political behavior divorced from rhetoric and constitutions.[3] He emphasized the role of groups and group interests in American politics, arguing that neither Fourth of July speeches about freedom nor constitutional language on the powers of the president is the engine that drives the American political system. Instead it is the interaction of political interests expressed by groups in the political system. Bentley's goal was to "fashion a tool" for this analysis.[4] His work prompted subsequent studies by Pendleton Herring, E.E. Schattschneider,[5] and others who eschewed the traditional study of political ideas and government institutions. Since then, group activity has been a major theme in political science.

The post-war study of political organizations dates from David B. Truman's seminal work, The Governmental Process, published in 1951. It prompted renewed attention to interest groups and other forms of non-electoral political organization.[6] Truman developed a theory of American politics that explains political outcomes as a meshing of interests expressed by the various groups in society. He directed attention to both organized and unorganized groups, which could be identified by their shared interests. Truman's influential work provoked an outpouring of studies of interest groups -- how they interact, express preferences, and form organized groups as institutionalized expressions of their interests.

Two of Truman's arguments have a special relevance for this work. First, he says that organized groups form during periods of stress or rapid changes, when people with shared interests interact more frequently. Second, he contends that behavioral and internal dynamics of political groups are "shared in their essential features, with non-political patterns of social interaction."[7] These claims are pivotal in studying the formation and behavior of political organizations, respectively.

Truman suggests a sociological model of groups emerging from "a disturbance in an institutional pattern ... or frustration in varying degrees of the habits of the participants, a circumstance that is always unpleasant and may be extremely painful."[8] Truman's claim is rooted in apparently rational patterns of behavior -- people respond to stress by seeking others with whom they can alleviate that stress.

Truman's assertion views political organizations as operating on essentially the same principles as non-political organizations. This leads him to borrow theoretically from anthropology, sociology, and organization theory,[9] and to use concepts developed in research on work organizations and bureaucracies. Many subsequent studies follow Truman's lead in this respect.

James Q. Wilson and Peter Clark, for example, apply general principles of organization to the study of political organizations.[10] They argue that all organizations "provide tangible or intangible incentives to individuals in exchange for contributions of individual activity to the organizations."[11] Their analysis borrows an incentive classification from Chester Barnard and claims that "much of the internal and external activity may be explained by understanding their incentive systems."[12]

Barnard, in his analysis of bureaucratic organizations,[13] identifies three basic types of incentives: material, solidary, and purposive. Material incentives are tangible rewards such as salary, tax benefits and the like. Solidary benefits are intangible socially-derived rewards, such as status, social interaction, and conviviality. Purposive incentives are motivations deriving from a desire to achieve a worthwhile goal. Clark and Wilson argue that this "incentive system may be regarded as the principal variable affecting organizational behavior."[14]

Other studies of political organization have challenged this approach, arguing instead that political organizations are unique and operate on their own principles. Mancur Olson, Jr., an economist, applied economic and marketing theory to Truman's analysis of political group formation. His analysis is strictly limited to economic interest groups and argued within an economic

3

rational choice model. However, he raises serious questions about Truman's sociological model of group formation.[19] Olson shows that it is not necessarily logical for people to respond to threats to their interests by contributing resources to an organization. His application of statistical analysis using rational economic models casts new light on the organization of interests and suggests that it is only reasonable to assume that political organizations will form under specific sets of circumstances.

Olson's argument rests on the distinction between collective and selective benefits. Collective benefits affect everyone equally. Selective benefits can be divided only among those who have contributed to their creation. Olson contends that individuals will not expend resources toward collective economic benefits expecting to "return a profit." People can be expected to join and contribute to an organization only when there is a positive balance of costs and benefits. Olson claims that the only ways to create such a balance are to (1) offer unrelated selective benefits to contributors, like group insurance; (2) apply legal coercion, as union shops and medical associations do; or (3) only organize small groups that are able to profit by their efforts.[16] Olson's analysis is of particular importance to low-income organizing, since success requires recruitment of relatively large numbers. Numerically, the Congress of Industrial Organizations, the most successful attempt to organize low-income Americans, did not really grow steadily until legal coercion was implemented in the form of the union shop. Even then, however, unions continued to provide selective benefits such as job-training, conviviality and newsletters.

Robert H. Salisbury's research on political organizations once again borrows from another discipline, operating from Truman's premise regarding the universality of organizational dynamics.[17] He applies exchange theory from sociology to devise a theoretical approach to political group formation and maintenance. He claims that a political organization is an exchange system in which an entrepreneur/organizer offers inducements to consumer/members to join, participate, and pay dues. His model is a more personalized variant of Olson's marketing concept. His approach is "neither true nor false but to be tested by its intellectual utility."[18] This approach provides historical insights by focusing on "origins and originators"[19] of organizations as calculated acts by rational actors.

The above studies have laid the groundwork of basic concepts and approaches to political organizations, borrowing from social psychology, anthropology, organization theory, economics, and marketing theory. Recently, several social scientists have tested and evaluated these theories using behavioral social science approaches. Two studies in particular, Terry Moe's The Organization of Interests[20] and David Knoke and James R. Wood's Organized for Action,[21] have used this approach to develop syntheses of the above theories backed by empirical social science arguments.

Moe's research focuses specifically on economic organizations and his model is based on Olson's analysis. He includes the Minnesota Farm Bureau Association, the Minnesota Farmers Union, the Minnesota Retail Association, the Minnesota-Dakotas Hardware Association and the Printing Industries of the Twin Cities, all economically oriented organizations that pursue their goals by political means -- principally lobbying. From his study, Moe offers revisions in Olson's theory of interest group formation that expand the scope of Olson's analysis to make the explanatory model "simple enough to clarify the nature of individual and organizational behavior, yet elaborate enough to address questions that are obviously important to a more comprehensive understanding."[22]

Moe's analysis addresses three pertinent areas: the decision individuals make to join, the organizational framework, and the internal politics of political organizations. The membership decision involves the prospective member's rationale for joining an organization. Moe argues that, in Olson's economic rationality model, the assumption of perfect knowledge of costs and benefits unduly restricts the applicability of his theory. In Moe's model, actors possess "bounded rationality," and "imperfect perception of the objective situation ..."[23] Moe retains the collective/selective distinction but expands the concept of benefits to include the types Clark and Wilson offer -- material, solidary, and purposive -- rather than strictly economic benefits. By increasing the complexity of individual motivation, Moe injects a clearly political dimension into the analysis that Olson fails to do.

The organizational side of Moe's analysis includes Salisbury's entrepreneur/leader concept, accompanied by staff and other paid personnel such as lobbyists and researchers. The entrepreneur focuses attention on "entrepreneurial options under varying conditions ..." and their effects on the organization.[24] Moe adds depth to the model by covering the internal politics of organizations and the degree to which their decision making processes include members, leaders and groups within the organizations.

Moe is eclectic in his choice of concepts and analytical techniques. He relies heavily on variations in Olson's analysis, yet expands it to make it more inclusive, to inject more of a political dimension, and to reflect more closely the kinds of organizations and phenomena one is likely to find in the political system.

> [O]nce we move beyond the idealized world of perfect information and economic self-interest, we are no longer led to Olson's non-political perspective. We are led, rather, to a broader view that leaves a good deal of room for political action and that outlines the theoretical roles of perceptions and values in explaining why political action occurs.[25]

Moe's model, for example, includes the possibility of an entrepreneur manipulating information critical to the decision to join. It is both possible and likely that entrepreneurs will both exaggerate members' efficacy and the value of benefits and minimize the costs of joining and participating, in order to persuade people to come into an organization. In this way, Moe seeks a median point in his analysis between the simple and theoretical, the complex and real.

Knoke and Wood emphasize the role of internal controls as a determinant of organizational success:

> The internal social control system plays an essential role in an organization's ability to acquire resources necessary to sustain collective life. Resources available to the organization, in turn, are crucial for the attainment of the group's external goals.[26]

Their organizational model highlights three important determinants for success: purposive incentives, opportunities to participate, and the legitimacy of leadership. They reason that an organization must mobilize its resources in order to achieve its goals. Mobilization occurs when the organizational control system can elicit commitment from membership and apply resources toward organizational goals. They find that

> Associations trying to develop high levels of

6

membership enthusiasm should try to foster all three conditions conducive to more effective organizational self-regulation: an emphasis on the purposive benefits from affiliation, widespread opportunities for membership participation in making important decisions, and ties to supralocal units that exercise formally legitimate restraints on local policy.[27]

By arguing for the importance of purposive incentives, Knoke and Wood favor the Truman approach to group organization. Their arguments for the importance of participation and legitimacy diverge from Olson's analysis of benefit distribution problems. Their findings, however, should not be seen as a refutation of Olson's claims, especially in light of what Moe argues: Olson's view is limited to a specific type of organization, and is further limited by his ideal economic model.

This discussion of political entrepreneurship and incentive theories of political organizations strongly suggests parallels between political organizing and product marketing. Olson's writing, in particular, develops analogies between these activities. It is therefore both analytically and practically useful to think of political organizations as marketable products. In this case study of ACORN, the market is low- and moderate-income citizens and the product is membership and participation in the political organization. Because of the peculiar nature of this market and product, I will develop a concept specific to political organizing: the idea of an "organizing strategy." The concept is familiar to community organizing professionals, and Moe uses the term at least once.[28]

An organizing strategy is a long-range plan for creating and maintaining a political organization. The components of an organizing strategy are: (1) the targeted constituency, (2) the terms of the exchange relationship between the group and its members, and (3) the organizational structure. Each component is dependent upon the others and plays a crucial role in the life of the organization. While the relationship between these organizational features holds in any kind of political organizing -- no matter the constituency or goals of the organizer/entrepreneur -- the concept of organizing strategy has not been fully articulated in the political science literature. It is so basic to so much of politics, however, that analysts have discussed parts of the concept, either directly or

7

indirectly; some have used the Salisbury thesis in this way.[29] But the notion has not been applied as explicitly as its centrality to political action demands.

Targeted constituency is the segment of the entire population from which a political organizer attempts to draw members. Many criteria are possible: sex, income, race, age, occupation, ideology, and so on. The choice of criteria shapes every other decision the entrepreneur makes, including the incentives to offer, resources to seek from members, organizational structure, and issue agenda.

Like the market in the economy, the constituency the entrepreneur chooses to attract determines the terms of exchange -- the benefits of membership, and what members give in return. The incentives the organizer offers must be suited to the tastes of the constituency, and therefore motivate prospective members to join, be active, and contribute resources. The constituents' status in society -- the role they play in the social, economic, and political spheres -- determines the resources they can most easily and effectively supply to the organization. Harry Spence, for example, notes that "The exercise of economic power by the poor to relieve their condition is foreclosed to them by definition. They have only the choice of political power or violence ..."[30] Thus, the organizer/entrepreneur must offer the targeted constituents something they need in return for something they have and can afford to expend.

Organizational form is the physical shape of the organization. It includes facets such as the size of constituent groups, the presence or absence of meetings, dues, the physical location of organizational headquarters, and so on. One need only consider the differences between community and workplace organizing or mailing list and grassroots organizing to appreciate the importance of this factor in an organizing strategy. This concept is not entirely distinct from the exchange relationship. For example, the higher the dues, the greater the demand made on the constituents. However, organizational structure does account for differences. For instance, different unit sizes change an organization's operation and its ability to attract and sustain members.

Thus, it is possible to distill the concept of "organizing strategy" from the literature on political organizations. The concepts of incentives, entrepreneurs, rational choice, and marketing strategy all suggest such an approach. Like a marketing strategy, however, an organizing strategy must suit its constituents, and some approaches are more fruitful than others.

The next chapter will discuss the kinds of organizing strategies that have been tried with low-income organizing. I use ACORN as a model, in the hope of shedding new light on political organizations in general. I will address questions such as:

1. Why do targeted constituents decide to join ACORN?

2. What kinds of incentives does ACORN use, and why?

3. Do the same incentives keep members active?

4. How do members perceive the purposive incentives the organization offers?

5. Are purposive incentives shared by members and organizers?

6. How important is members' participation in the decision making process?

7. What role does the organizational structure play in the success or failure?

Notes to Chapter I

[1]*The People Decide*, Program of the ACORN National Platform Conference, St. Louis, June 30-July 1, 1979, pp. 10-16.

[2]Iver Peterson, "Glimpse of 'Real Detroit' Given to 13 Republicans," *New York Times*, 13 July, 1980, p. 12.

[3]Arthur F. Bentley, *The Process of Government* (Cambridge, MA: The Belknap Press, 1967).

[4]Ibid., n.p.

[5]Pendleton Herring, *Group Representation Before Congress* (Baltimore: Johns Hopkins Univ. Press, 1929); E.E. Schattschneider, *Politics, Pressures, and the Tariff* (New York: Prentice-Hall, Inc., 1935).

[6]David B. Truman, *The Governmental Process* (New York: Alfred A. Knopf, 1962).

[7]Ibid., p. ix.

[8]Ibid., p. 29.

[9]Ibid., pp. 18 ff.

[10]Peter B. Clark and James Q. Wilson, "Incentive Systems: A Theory of Organizations," Administrative Science Quarterly 6 (1961), p. 129.

[11]Ibid., p. 130.

[12]Ibid.

[13]Chester I. Barnard, The Functions of the Executive (Cambridge, MA: Harvard Univ. Press, 1938).

[14]Clark and Wilson, p. 130.

[15]Mancur Olson, The Logic of Collective Action (Cambridge, MA: Harvard Univ. Press, 1977).

[16]Ibid., p. 2.

[17]Robert H. Salisbury, "An Exchange Theory of Interest Groups," Midwest Journal of Political Science 13 (Feb., 1969), p. 1.

[18]Ibid., p. 31.

[19]Ibid., p. 29.

[20]Terry M. Moe, The Organization of Interests (Chicago: Univ. of Chicago Press, 1980).

[21]David Knoke and James R. Wood, Organized for Action (New Brunswick, NJ: Rutgers Univ. Press, 1981).

[22]Moe, p. 5.

[23]Ibid., p. 18.

[24]Ibid., p. 20.

[25]Ibid., p. 537.

[26]Knoke and Wood, p. 2.

[27]Ibid., pp. 109-110.

[28]Moe, p. 40.

[29]James Q. Wilson, _Political Organizations_ (New York: Basic Books, Inc., 1973), pp. 30 ff.; Moe, pp. 36 ff.

[30]Robert Lovinger, "Can Harry Spence Fix Public Housing?" _The Boston Globe Magazine_ (23 August, 1981), p. 44.

C H A P T E R   I I

PRINCIPLES OF LOW-INCOME ORGANIZING

Major studies of political participation show a clear, consistent and strong correlation between socioeconomic status (SES) and membership in political organizations: higher income and upper status citizens participate more, both quantitatively and qualitatively, than do those at the other end of the income and status continuum.[1] While many studies document the relationship between SES and group membership, Sidney Verba and Norman H. Nie explore the implications of that relationship for public policy and power relationships. They find, in cross-national studies, that the correlation between political participation and SES in the U.S. is as high or higher than in any of the other nations studied.[2] For example, 57% of the respondents who scored in the highest one-sixth category of participation on their scale were in the upper third of the SES index; only 14% of them were from the lowest third.[3] Hence, the upper SES people who participate at the highest rates numerically outnumber the lower two-thirds SES group.

It is not a statistical sleight-of-hand that makes SES and political participation seem so closely connected. As Verba and Nie explain, the "relationship that looks so moderate from some perspectives (the correlation between our SES and participation scales is, after all, only .37) is in fact a quite striking one from the point of view of what it implies about the composition of a population."[4]

Verba and Nie speculate as to whether group membership increases or decreases the impact of SES on political participation. They find that for an individual, group membership increases the amount of participation more for low SES participants than for high SES participants. Given the higher rate of membership among upper SES citizens, the overall effect of group membership in American politics is to "push in the direction of increasing the disparity"[5] of influence between class.

Table 2-1 illustrates the organizational activity of people in different SES categories:

13

TABLE 2-1

PROPORTIONS ORGANIZATIONALLY ACTIVE IN LOWER, MIDDLE,
AND UPPER THIRD OF SES (in percent)[6]

	Lower SES	Middle SES	Upper SES	Total
Nonmember	56	34	20	38
Passive Member	23	22	21	22
Single Active	16	28	24	22
Multiple Active	6	16	35	19
Total	100	100	100	100

Verba and Nie's findings strongly suggest that lack of participation in political organizations by lower SES groups reduces their influence on the public policies that affect their lives.

Truman's sociological model of group formation is problematic for the study of low-income organizations. He argues that political organizations emerge in times of stress, but low-income Americans are in a more or less continual state of distress, yet join organizations in lower numbers than higher income Americans. Truman points out that while low-income people suffer unemployment and other economic dislocations, their low rate of political participation leaves them no organized channels through which to express grievances. This increases the potential for radical political movements, which have not internalized the prevailing political folkways that encourage stability in the political system. Short of a radical outcome, Truman believes that government will continue to be skewed in favor of upper-income citizens at the expense of lower-income interest.[7] The lower rate of low-income participation in political organizations thus both renders the political system less stable and denies a major portion of society equal opportunity to express its political interests.

The concern of political analysts over the low rate of participation among low-income Americans spans the political spectrum. The question of how to attract and maintain low-income members is of critical importance to both conservatives and leftist organizers, although for different reasons. It is a widespread belief among leftists that the way to achieve social justice in American politics is through sustained, organized political power of the lower classes; this has led, among other things, to their support for the labor movement. Saul Alinsky premised his early organizing and writing on this idea.

Conservatives have also considered ways to build organizational ties among low-income Americans as a way to stem anomie and potentially destructive radical mass movements. However, social scientists do not agree about the most effective way to organize low-income people. To understand both the debate and the potential to organize low-income people, we must first examine the common explanations for the difficulties encountered in organizing low-income people.

Organizational Problems in Low-Income Organizing

Almond and Verba, as well as Verba and Nie, suggest hypotheses to explain the lower rate of organizational membership among lower-income respondents. They suggest that factors contributing to upper SES activism might include higher levels of social and organizational skills, socialization processes that encourage group activity, greater resources like time and money, stimulation by their active SES cohorts, and a higher sense of their political efficacy. However, it is difficult to determine the flow of relationships. For example, which of the following most accurately depicts reality?

1 -- SES -> EFFICACY -> GROUP MEMBERSHIP

2 -- SES -> GROUP MEMBERSHIP -> EFFICACY

3 -- SES -> GROUP MEMBERSHIP
     ↘   ↓
        EFFICACY

Available survey data does not permit clear determination of the causal flow. Verba and Nie, for example, qualify their claim that "organizations do have an independent effect over and above any such general propensity toward activity," because "participation proneness" can only be measured indirectly.[8] They most clearly connect low-income group membership to political participation and political outcomes in the U.S. when they point out that in other political systems, group membership's effects on political participation do not exaggerate upper-income political influence.

> Participation, looked at generally, does not
> necessarily help one social group rather than
> another. The general model of the sources and
> consequences of participation that we have
> presented could work in a number of ways. It

15

> could work so that lower-status citizens were
> more effective politically and used that
> political effectiveness to improve their social
> and economic circumstances. Or it could work,
> as it appears to do in the United States, to
> benefit upper-status citizens more. It depends
> on what organizations, parties, and belief
> systems exist, and how these all effect
> participation rates. Participation remains a
> powerful social force increasing or decreasing
> inequality. It depends on who takes advantage
> of it.[9]

Hence, those seeking political equality would do well to engage low-income people actively in voluntary organizations, especially those that deal with community problems and political issues. This requires an understanding of the problems encountered in low-income organizing; the political organization literature provides limited guidance in this area.

Wilson's _Political Organizations_[10] argues that low-income citizens are best organized around material incentives, solidary incentives that provide "opportunities for vivid and uninhibited expansion of core lifestyles," and purposive incentives that "involve personal and intense, not anonymous or vicarious experience."[11] He claims too that low-income activists operate in a relatively shorter time frame than do upper-income activists.[12] That claim is echoed by Saul Alinsky and others who have studied the organizational politics of low-income citizens.[13]

As a result of this shorter time frame, low-income activists need to be constantly working on issues, or else member activism diminishes. Thus, the combination of incentive types and shorter time frame requires political organizations of low-income citizens to produce a stable supply of what Sherry Arnstein terms "deliverables,"[14] i.e., outcomes of political demands expressed by the organization and conceded by government or other opponents in the political system. Arnstein's analysis closely parallels Alinsky's contention that low-income organizing requires the delivery of "wins" that are quickly achieved and yield visible benefits wrested from political and economic institutions.[15] Without a steady supply of "deliverables," both Arnstein and Alinsky believe that building a political organization of low-income citizens is virtually impossible. Hence, an organizer of low-income people must include ways and means of procuring such benefits on a regular basis. This leads Alinsky to enunciate three basic tenets of community organizing: (1) issues must be winnable; (2) tactics must entail confrontation; and (3) the organizing process must provide opportunities to express anger and overcome fear.

Although these analyses yield useful insights into participation of low SES individuals, none of them adequately explores the perspectives of the groups least likely to participate in political decision making: racial minorities and low-income people. A full study of why certain groups in the system are participating far less regularly and effectively should examine the experiences and perceptions of those groups more carefully. It should also examine the integral relationship between power and participation. A recent study of politics and power in Appalachia by John Gaventa takes this approach.[16]

Gaventa's analysis is a study of power. He argues that neither the pluralists nor their critics explain enough about the relations between the powerful and the powerless, nor does either adequately identify the causes of class differences in participation rates. He claims that there are three dimensions of power in American politics, the first treated by the pluralists, the second by the critics of pluralism, and the third primarily by sociologists like C. Wright Mills and Steven Lukes.[17]

The pluralists, Gaventa argues, accurately depict power struggles in American politics, but only those that pit reasonably evenly matched opponents within decision making institutions. These struggles, based on democratic principles of conflict, involve opposing arrays of strategies and resources applied in public policy settings. When an issue arises between less evenly matched opponents, however, the stronger side is able to deny the other side access to decision making institutions -- thus preventing an issue from being placed on the political agenda. Schattschneider describes this second level of power analysis as the "mobilization of bias." Gaventa, however, sees a "third face of power."

The third dimension of power exists when power resources are so highly skewed in favor of one group that they are able to go beyond "bias." This third face of power is more extreme. It "influences, shapes, or determines conceptions of the necessities, possibilities, and strategies of challenge in situations of latent conflict."[18] Hence, powerless people do not challenge the status quo; they accept it as legitimate and inevitable. Gaventa suggests a number of processes by which powerholders maintain consensus through apathy and quiescence of the powerless, in spite of powerless people's obvious self-interest in change: (1) controlling information and manipulating symbols; (2) instilling fatalism by consistently denying opposing claims; (3) denying the benefits of participation, including political education; and (4) manipulating emerging attempts to challenge the status quo.[19]

The third dimension of power works as follows: (1) public and private institutions withhold as much information as possible and couch their arguments as defending free enterprise against "creeping socialism"; (2) the low-income activists are easily intimidated because they have no experience or tradition of political victory to bolster them; (3) the activists' convictions are weak, lacking the broad education of a background in political activism and experience exercising their rights in a democratic society;[20] and (4) for the above reasons, the activists are easily intimidated and misled by the arguments and strategies of their opponents. Thus, Gaventa, unlike either the pluralists or Schattschneider, explains in testable terms the exclusion of large portions of the populace from the political process.

Gaventa applies his theory of power relations to an explanation of apathy and quiescence among people in Appalachia who clearly receive disproportionately few benefits from society. In his view, it is not a matter of cultural values, consensus, or a lack of resources -- as pluralists claim[21] -- nor merely the mobilization of bias successfully excluding them. Rather, "power serves to maintain [the] prevailing order of inequality ... through the shaping of beliefs about the order's legitimacy or immutability."[22] This makes it difficult to organize low-income citizens into unions, welfare rights organizations, or groups like ACORN. Robert Botsch, for example, interviewed North Carolina furniture workers who objected to union organizing despite the clear benefits of increased wages, safer working conditions, and the fairer work practices they agreed unions provide, and concluded that people who have been dominated tend to lose sight of the possibility for change.[23]

In his analysis of power, Gaventa offers a process by which powerless groups might build the power to bargain and compete successfully in a genuinely pluralist fashion. His theory is essentially a reversal of the three dimensions of power; groups develop a "consciousness of the needs, possibilities, and strategies of change";[24] then, they must "overcome the mobilization of bias";[25] and finally, they must develop resources with which to conduct political action in decision making areas of the first dimension of power. In fact, Gaventa claims, genuine participation takes place only in: "self-determined action with others similarly affected upon clearly conceived and articulated grievances."[26]

Gaventa's prescription for arriving at that point and his analysis of the dimensions of power suggest the basic tenets of community organizing. First, winnability is crucial, because a "single victory helps to alter inaction owing to the anticipation of defeat, leading to more action, and so on. Once patterns of quiescence are broken upon one set of grievances, the accumulating resources of challenge -- e.g., organization, momentum, consciousness -- may become transferable to other issues and other targets."[27]

Second, confrontational tactics -- "to err on the side of too much action" -- help to overcome institutional barriers against low-income activism. Confrontation gives institutional leaders reason to include the activists -- to avoid being subjected to confrontational politics. Clearly, if an organization of low-income activists has effective access to an institution's decision making process, it will not take the trouble to fill meeting rooms with raucous, shouting protestors.

However, if members do confront, they experience resistance which demonstrates for the politically uninitiated the effectiveness of institutional barriers in preventing grievances from being aired in the institutional agenda. The members who learn this lesson not only can work to bring down those barriers, but perceive other obstacles more readily.

Finally, low-income activists who have dealt effectively with their anger and fear are better prepared to use their available resources more effectively in power struggles with government and corporate leaders. At that point, Dahl's advice in After the Revolution? is appropriate:

> In order for those who are politically weak to push through a crucial if still incompleted process of democratization, they have to learn how to pyramid their political resources very much in the way that, in the economic realm, an aggressive young man-on-the-make sometimes arranges to transform his personal situation from poverty to riches.[28]

Before that, however, resources, energy, strategy and organization must all be focused on the highly unequal struggle to achieve some degree of political parity on the road from quiescence to meaningful activism. In addition to the special problems that Wilson and others cite in organizing low-income people, Gaventa argues that pre-existing power relations are a critical factor in determining organizing tactics. According to Gaventa, the three dimensions of power determine the course of any organizing projects by requiring the three techniques mentioned above. Clearly, they are mainstays of low-income organizing. There are, moreover, other considerations that help determine the most desirable organizing strategies to use in low-income organizing.

Constraints and Available Choices

There are constraints on the organizing strategy that an organizer must accept. Constituents cannot give what they do not have, will only respond to meaningful incentives, and require a profitable exchange before they will join and maintain an organization. The resources the organizer wishes to offer must be available in some form at a price that "customers" are willing to pay. In addition, the organizational form the organizer adopts must suit both the constituents and the resources the organization seeks to offer.

Richard Rich describes a "political economy" of community organizations that delineates many of the constraints community organizations face.[29] He argues that the two major costs are decision making costs and deprivation costs.[30] Decision making costs are the resources expended in collective decision making, while deprivation costs are the price of "being bound by group decisions that run counter to their [individual] preferences."[31]

The decision making process with the highest cost is the unanimity rule; it requires much more effort to achieve unanimous agreement than majority agreement to binding decisions. The highest deprivation costs are experienced in oligarchical groups in which a small leadership cadre makes and enforces binding decisions on the membership, as work organizations do.

The interplay of these factors means that the rational choice for communities with few resources and high demands is to remain unorganized and risk nothing, or to adopt an "exit choice," i.e., allow for an option to quit. Both of these would minimize both types of costs.[32] "From the individual's short-term perspective," Rich argues, "voluntarism may be a highly rational response to the resource situation of poor citizens, even though it may handicap the community in the long run."[33] Thus, minimizing risk-taking for individuals and making the decision to join more attractive weakens the organization that may subsequently be created.

The need to form voluntary organizations with exit choices in low-income neighborhoods leads to an increase in the costs of organizational maintenance and the reliance on selective and purposive incentives as substitutes for coercion.[34] Rich compares neighborhood groups from communities of varying SES and finds that the higher the SES, the greater the likelihood that coercive organizations -- property owner groups and community development organizations -- will exist. The greatest concentration of neighborhood organizations of any kind was in middle-income neighborhoods, since low-income neighborhoods are handicapped by the dynamics described above and upper-income neighborhoods reflect individualist strategies to meet residential needs. In addition to the higher maintenance costs of the voluntary organizations, Rich found that coercive organizations were more effective in obtaining collective material goods for their neighborhoods.[35] Hence, Rich argues that the choices available to low-income neighborhoods are limited and not very attractive. Moreover, they impose additional constraints on the organizer.

It is generally agreed among those studying voluntary organizations that the problems posed by Olson regarding rational choices in pursuit of collective action, require organizers to adopt two somewhat contradictory strategies: purposive incentives and maximum constituent participation.[36] This dynamic is particularly true of low-income organizations, where (1) purposive incentives are easily obtainable, while material goods are not, and (2) the lack of material resources requires that low-income constituents contribute their labor to the organization.

Moe argues that these dynamics conflict, since purposive incentives or ideology increase the power of professional staff and frequently displace the goal of organization-building.[37] He argues that the staff "who control political information and expertise and perform valuable political services will find they have a stronger basis for influence."[38] Goal displacement occurs when "the group's goals are not a means to ... ends, but are ends in themselves that take on value because of their ideological nature; they are, from the entrepreneur's standpoint,

the raison d'etre of the association."[39] When goal
displacement occurs, Moe argues, "entrepreneurs" or organizers
attempt to prevent constituent input into goal-setting by
developing other incentive structures, propagandizing,
manipulating group activities toward group goals only, and hiring
staff according to their beliefs rather than their
competence.[40]

Constraints therefore pose real problems for organizers
attempting to build low-income organizations. They force
organizers to rely on voluntary organizations, develop purposive
incentives, and stimulate massive constituent participation.
Determining how to accommodate these constraints, however, is
only the first set of choices to be made.

Available Choices

Of course the idea of constraints on choices of organizing
strategies is theoretical. Organizers have historically chosen a
wide variety of exchange relationships and organizational forms
with varying degrees of success. To develop further the notion
of organizing strategy and to delineate the available options, we
will examine different organizing strategies that have been
attempted with low-income constituents.

One of the more closely studied organizing strategies for
low-income constituents is that of the National Welfare Rights
Organization (NWRO). The constituency of the short-lived NWRO
was welfare recipients -- mostly female, black, and clearly
low-income. Lawrence Bailis found that NWRO members had an
especially intense dependence upon government service agencies
for their livelihood and that many were not receiving nearly the
amount of government benefits to which they were entitled. This
clear and easily remedied gap between entitlements and benefits
provided a unique opportunity for organizers of the NWRO. It
offered the chance to obtain "tangible benefits that are quickly
realizable."[41] An exchange relationship could thereby be
created in which material incentives were offered to members by
the organizer's ability to manipulate welfare entitlement
regulations. Concurrently, the organization made only minimal
demands on its constituency. As Bailis put it, "demands on the
membership should be minimized: the less asked, the better."[42]

The organizational form of the NWRO was simple. The
organizers developed lists of welfare recipients by any means
they could and contacted prospective constituents to persuade
them that they could obtain increased benefits through the NWRO.

The organizers then staged a mass meeting of recipients in a local church or hall and elected pre-appointed officers by acclamation. Then they took the meeting to the local welfare office to demand supplementary benefits for items such as furniture, winter clothing, and other poorly publicized special grants written into welfare legislation.

Dues were one dollar per year, used largely as a token of members' contribution and an expression of commitment. Dues also accommodated the standard organizational rituals involving lobbying claims and inquiries regarding funding sources.[43] Finally, although individual NWRO chapters lasted less than a year, during that time, organizers maintained "intensive and continuing personal contact" with the members.[44] For the most part, the groups were loose, short-lived, closely managed by staff, and based largely on personal relations between members and staff.

Nationally, the NWRO could not sustain itself long either. The source of its incentives -- the special grants from the welfare offices -- dried up when state legislatures instituted flat grant systems of benefits. Other strategies, such as advocacy and grievances, were insufficient to maintain the organization, since recipients of such benefits from the NWRO no longer had reason to stay in the organization when their problem was resolved. The only purposive incentive attempted was to convey the belief that "[t]he reason welfare is so bad is because welfare recipients are not organized. One by one they can't get what they need because they have no power -- and that's what this country responds to, power."[45] Any ideological articulation beyond that was eschewed: the NWRO organizers "put down attempts at ideological justification for a course of action as 'radical bullshit'."[46] Nor, as their organizing strategy dictated, did the NWRO attempt to stimulate constituent participation. Rather, they made as few demands as possible in order to keep the benefit/cost ratio as high as possible.

The NWRO was therefore incapable of developing or maintaining incentives adequate to the constituents it sought to organize. Material benefits had only a short-term effectiveness, and the organizers chose not to develop members' commitment through participation or purposive incentives. The combination of targeted constituency, exchange relationship, and organizational form was not effective in the environment in which it was attempted. While a single case does not prove a rule, it is clear that this organizing strategy did not operate within the constraints outlined above, and consequently failed.

Another organizing strategy that has been widely attempted is Saul Alinsky's technique of community organizing. Unlike the NWRO, as Joan Lancourt has shown,[47] Alinsky's groups sometimes lasted for many years, rescuing several communities from urban blight and providing long-term services to community residents. Alinsky organizers targeted leaders of local community organizations within low- and moderate-income neighborhoods. These included religious leaders, block club officers, people in business organizations, and officers of ethnic organizations. Alinsky and his organizers tried to enroll these leaders and their organizations as constituent groups under umbrella organizations set up by Alinsky.

The exchange relationship between organizer and constituents was more varied and intense than the NWRO's. Alinsky groups offered immediate, tangible incentives to their constituents, such as jobs, fair treatment at the local supermarket, and improved city services. Longer-term goals of Alinsky groups included establishing services such as Community Development Corporations and protecting neighborhoods from urban redevelopment and freeway construction.

The purposive incentives offered were the ideals of democratic participation in the political system for the local community leadership. The intended result of the incentive system was to enable "each intermediate or short-term struggle to broaden the participants' consciousness, propelling them on to the next set of issues. Without this clear, overall perspective, which imbues individual victories with a larger significance, the benefits of each advance, no matter how valuable ..., may dissipate, overwhelmed by the new problems arising from the ever-changing reality."[48] Hence, the incentive system is structured to expand the constituent commitment and understanding from the immediate and concrete to the more distant and idealistic.

Alinsky groups made greater demands on constituents than the NWRO. Alinsky confrontation techniques required members to picket, rally, and protest at times, and to support local institutions such as the Community Development Corporations at others. Lancourt points out that the demands on leaders were far greater than on members of the constituents' groups.[49] Compared to the NWRO, however, participants in Alinsky groups were asked to provide a great deal more of the resources necessary for organization-building and achievement of community goals.

24

PRINCIPLES OF LOW-INCOME ORGANIZING

The organizational form of the Alinsky groups, as noted above, is the federated umbrella structure. The dues payers are constituent groups -- churches, ethnic organizations, and block clubs. The boards of the Alinsky groups consist of leaders of the constituent groups who meet regularly and make the important decisions about group goals and strategies. The boards receive a great deal of guidance from the organizers early in the process but the organizers withdraw after a pre-determined period of time -- usually four years.

The Alinsky groups generally stay within the constraints outlined above. They exercise some important options regarding constituency and organizational form. They also consciously apply a progression of incentives designed to develop the allegiance and sophistication of their constituents. They also demand a fair degree of participation from constituents, as Moe argues is necessary. While that increases the cost of participation, the relative success of Alinsky groups versus the NWRO suggests this was a good strategic choice.

There is no consensus on the most effective means of organizing low- and moderate-income people for political action. There are principles and techniques that have been developed and some rules guiding their use given the constraints of different settings. But there is no one right way. I will examine further the organizing strategies of low-income groups, specifically the organizing strategy of the Boston chapter of ACORN.

Notes to Chapter II

[1] Lester W. Milbrath, _Political Participation_ (Chicago: Rand McNally and Co., 1965), p. 132; and Sidney Verba and Norman Nie, _Participation in America_ (New York: Harper and Row, 1972), pp. 181 and 204.

[2] Verba and Nie, p. 340.

[3] Ibid., p. 131.

[4] Ibid.

[5] Ibid., p. 204.

[6] Ibid.

[7] David B. Truman, _The Governmental Process_ (New York:

Alfred A. Knopf, 1962), p. 522.

[8]Verba and Nie, p. 200.

[9]Ibid., p. 342.

[10]James Q. Wilson, Political Organizations (New York: Basic Books, Inc., 1973).

[11]Ibid., p. 73.

[12]Ibid., p. 62.

[13]Si Kahn, Organizing (New York: McGraw-Hill Book Co., 1982), p. 168.

[14]Sherry Arnstein, "Maximum Feasible Manipulation," Public Administration Review 32 (Sept., 1972), pp. 377-402.

[15]Saul D. Alinsky, Reveille for Radicals (New York: Vintage Books, 1969), p. 175.

[16]John Gaventa, Power and Powerlessness (Urbana, IL: Univ. of Illinois Press, 1980).

[17]C. Wright Mills, The Power Elite (New York: Oxford Univ. Press, 1959); and Steven Lukes, Power (Cambridge, U.K.: Cambridge Univ. Press, 1970).

[18]Gaventa, p. 15.

[19]Ibid., pp. 19-20.

[20]Carole Pateman, Participation and Democratic Theory (Cambridge, U.K.: Cambridge Univ. Press, 1979), p. 15.

[21]Gaventa, pp. 40-42.

[22]Ibid., p. 42.

[23]Robert Botsch, We Shall Not Overcome (Chapel Hill, NC: Univ. of North Carolina Press, 1981).

[24]Gaventa, p. 24.

[25]Ibid.

[26]Ibid.

[27]Ibid., p. 25.

[28]Robert Dahl, After the Revolution? (New Haven: Yale Univ. Press, 1975), p. 106.

[29]Richard C. Rich, "A Political-Economy Approach to the Study of Neighborhood Organizations," American Journal of Political Science 4 (Nov., 1980), pp. 559-591.

[30]Ibid., p. 565.

[31]Ibid.

[32]Ibid., p. 566.

[33]Ibid., p. 578.

[34]Ibid., p. 570.

[35]Ibid., p. 572.

[36]Terry M. Moe, The Organization of Interest (Chicago: Univ. of Chicago Press, 1980); and David Knoke and James R. Wood, Organized for Action (New Brunswick, NJ: Rutgers Univ. Press, 1981).

[37]Moe, pp. 134-136.

[38]Ibid., p. 134.

[39]Ibid., p. 135.

[40]Ibid., p. 136.

[41]Bill Pastreich and Rhoda Linton, "The Boston Model," a mimeograph paper quoted in Lawrence Neil Bailis, Bread or Justice (Lexington, MA: D.C. Heath and Co., 1974), p. 19.

[42]Bailis, p. 21.

[43]Ibid., p. 40.

[44]Ibid., p. 21.

[45]Pastreich and Linton, p. 40.

[46]Bailis, p. 91.

[47]Joan E. Lancourt, <u>Confront</u> <u>or</u> <u>Concede</u> (Lexington, MA: D.C. Heath and Co., 1979).

[48]Ibid., p. 35.

[49]Ibid., p. 121.

C H A P T E R   I I I

THE ACORN ORGANIZING STRATEGY

ACORN's organizing strategy for low-income people lends itself to analysis because it is clearly articulated and recorded in a variety of places. The founder of ACORN, Wade Rathke, drafted this plan before he began his work. Rathke designed a strategy that could be executed and replicated throughout the country. He has discussed his plan in a variety of sources, including memos, news articles, and commentaries on organizing techniques. Moreover, he has cited the sources that inspired his organizing plan. For these reasons, we can easily apply our analysis of organizing strategy to the ACORN organization.

When Rathke began the organization in 1970, he was working as an organizer for the Massachusetts Welfare Rights Organization (MWRO), a branch of the NWRO. He developed a plan to organize a majority constituency using techniques that would mobilize lower class Americans. He promoted the idea with the MWRO and received a grant to go to Little Rock, Arkansas, to create such an organization. Rathke described his goal:

> With the welfare issue, you're always dealing with a minority. We all knew that we had to break out of the single-issue campaign. I wanted to build on a majority constituency rather than on a minority, where the next-door neighbors are in it together, not fighting each other.[1]

Hence, Rathke clearly fits the Salisbury model of an organizer/entrepreneur, selling an organization to a group in the political system.

Rathke provides the sources of ideas for his organizing strategy. The nature of the sources and the manner in which Rathke blended them shows both his intentions and social priorities. All of the sources of ideas were organizations attempting to organize low-income people. The Civil Rights

Movement developed the ideas of using confrontational tactics, as did Saul Alinsky's community organizing. Fred Ross of the United Farm Workers developed the notion of house meetings "to build a sense of community among potential organization members ..."[2] The membership dues system started with the labor movement and the Non-Partisan League of North Dakota.[3] The notion of training and supporting professional organizers was also a product of Non-Partisan League organizing. Finally, the idea of developing a clearly articulated model and applying it in neighborhoods across the country was inspired by the Boston Model of the NWRO, created by Rhoda Linton and Bill Pastreich.

The Boston Model was used as "the basis for NWRO's ability to send raw white organizers ... into Minnesota, Ohio, Illinois, Rhode Island, and New York and, in a matter of months, produce organization."[4] Rathke, the former NWRO organizer, devised a similar organizing strategy designed for a majority constituency. Because the plan is inspired by previous attempts to solve specific prior organizing problems, we can identify what Rathke saw as the relevant problems and the most suitable solutions, i.e., how to create and sustain a political organization of low- and moderate-income citizens in American politics.

Like the Boston Model, the ACORN organizing strategy is designed to be implemented and replicated anywhere in the country. This reinforces the similarity to a marketing strategy consciously designed to appeal to a specific constituency within the political system. The strategy has been applied for over fifteen years in both urban and rural settings, in twenty-six states, plus the District of Columbia. Clearly, the strategy can survive many of the problems of low-income organizing cited in the previous chapter.

Finally, the goal that Rathke set for ACORN, "Power to the People," makes clear the intention of its founder and provides a guide for evaluating its success. In more formal terms, Rathke describes the organization's goal in the beginning of his detailed memo entitled "ACORN Community Organizing Model":

> GOAL: To build a mass community organization which has as its primary principle the development of sufficient organizational power to achieve its individual members' interests, its local objectives, and in connection with other groups, its state interests. The organization must be permanent with

> multi-issued concerns achieved through
> multi-tacticed [sic] direct action, and
> membership participating in policy, financing,
> and achievement of group goals and community
> improvements.[5]

The model, when applied in neighborhoods across the country, aims
at building a national organization made up of the local chapters
which can "deal with the manifestations of power in whatever form
they take."[6] When local groups coordinate their efforts,
Rathke believes, they can redistribute power in the American
political system to the ACORN constituency.

The Targeted Constituency

The targeted constituency in the ACORN organizing strategy
is a majority of the American people. Writing in 1975 with
Steven Kest in the ACORN Organizing Handbook #2, Rathke stated:

> it is imperative that ACORN see as its
> constituency all the people in this country who
> are shut out of ... power. As a rough working
> guide ACORN has traditionally defined this
> constituency as consisting of those of low to
> moderate income. By any standards you hit
> upon, that constituency contains within it a
> majority of the people in this country. It is
> that majority that is going to have to be
> organized if there is any hope for changing --
> for reversing -- the prevailing distribution of
> power.[7]

Hence, the constituency that Rathke targeted is defined by its
income and lack of power. ACORN includes all racial groups; the
criterion of income has remained essentially consistent.

Member recruitment is organized by neighborhood. Since
neighborhoods are heterogeneous in their economic makeup, some
members may be relatively well off. ACORN chooses target
neighborhoods through a variety of considerations:

> Either ACORN is invited into a neighborhood by
> some of its residents, or the Executive Board
> picks, for various strategic reasons, a
> neighborhood to be organized. The Board might
> chose a neighborhood because it is in a city
> council ward where ACORN isn't as strong as it

31

would like to be; or because the racial or
income character of the neighborhood will help
give the overall organization its vital
balances; or because an important issue that
might affect the whole area (a new highway, for
example) is making its first appearance in that
neighborhood.[8]

Thus, the choice may be either tactical or demographic but
historically, the basic determinant has been income. Gary
Delgado's study of ACORN's membership found that, of 50,000
members, 70% are "black and Latino, 70% female, and almost all
from the working class ..."[9]

The Exchange Relationship

"Deliverables." ACORN organizers seek members from their
low- and moderate-income constituency who will contribute time
and resources. In pursuit of those members, they initially offer
the "deliverables" described in the previous chapter. Organizers
are instructed on how to develop and pursue such issues in each
neighborhood. The initial organizing drive that creates the
individual neighborhood groups -- virtually every ACORN group is
started fresh by ACORN organizers -- begins the exchange process.

The Organizing Model describes the process by which
organizers seek issues that will interest prospective members:

Driving or walking through a neighborhood you
can often spot visible issues -- streets, open
ditches, drainage, bad lighting, condemned or
dilapidated housing, curbs, gutters, sidewalks,
litter, domestic and commercial eyesores, weeds
and overgrown lots, lack of parks or
recreational facilities, bus routes, and a
number of other issues. Depending on the
situations, all of these things are potential
organizing issues.[10]

While seeking issues that are winnable and relatively easy to
achieve, the organizer must also discuss what the residents
perceive as the most important issues in the neighborhood.

At the beginning of an organizing drive, neighborhood
residents may identify issues through two basic means: the
"Organizing Committee" and the residents canvassed in their
homes. The Organizing Committee is a cadre of twelve to twenty

32

people who are the core of the organization during the drive. They usually consist of people who have contacted ACORN requesting that a group be organized in their neighborhood, friends of those contacts, or people known to the contacts as interested in political activity.[11] They provide legitimacy for the drive and become leaders in the organizing work; they are often the original officers of the group. Canvassing, or "doorknocking," allows the organizer and members of the Organizing Committee to contact as many of the people in the neighborhood as possible before the "First Meeting," or initial neighborhood-wide meeting. The interaction "on the doors" is critical to the success of the drive and is where a great deal of the "salesmanship" for the organization occurs. The Model states:

> There is no substitute for personal contact in convincing people to become active in the organization. Doorknocking does it best. It gives the doorknockers a chance to answer questions and create the impressions of the organization. It allows you to bring people in, and define some people out.[12]

In each relatively brief interaction (fifteen minutes is recommended), the doorknocker learns what the residents think about the neighborhood and what issues they consider important. It is an unusually direct interaction between citizen and political organizer, and occurs with nearly a thousand residents in each neighborhood organized.

Typically, the issues with which the organizers begin are relatively easy to identify: clearing vacant lots, obtaining needed traffic control, open ditches, and so on. In most cases, a visit to a city official is all that is needed to obtain satisfaction for the residents. These "wins" are tangible, quite visible, and provide clear proof of success for the local organizing drive. In organizational terms, the deliverables can be defined as collective material benefits, i.e., they are tangible and all of the residents of the neighborhood benefit regardless of whether they pay dues or participate in ACORN. Thus, ACORN organizers rely on material collective incentives to launch new groups and recruit members. They do not deal significantly with the problems of free riders or maintaining supplies of accessible "deliverables."

Non-purposive Selective Incentives. Three types of non-ideological selective incentives are available: material, camaraderie, and status. Surprisingly, in light of the political organization literature, ACORN's organizing strategy does not mention the social incentives, and does not treat selective material incentives as critical to organization building. While it is difficult to conceive of an organization that does not offer any social incentives in practice, ACORN does not cultivate that type of incentive in its model or its literature. The Organizing Model discusses arranging discounts from local merchants for ACORN members. But it does not discuss discounts as a means of attracting members; rather, it states that discounts make "it easier to build legitimacy with your community contacts ..."[13] The types of selective material incentives offered by ACORN groups around the country, such as oil co-ops, are not intended to be primary motivations for members to join or remain involved in ACORN. The main reliance is on purposive incentives. Organizers ground their appeal on the organization's goals.

Purposive Incentives. Political ideology includes the kinds of world views epitomized by liberals, conservatives, and socialists. In that realm, one might expect low-income organizers to espouse and apply leftist ideologies. However, this is not always the case. As Fainstein and Fainstein discovered, urban political activists are sometimes forced into a position of opposing liberal ideals:

> While the costs of attacking "liberal" institutions may be high, their salience to the lives of ghetto inhabitants is great; Congress or big business might be more important causative factors in the situation of the poor, but they are much less visible and much less the immediate creators of the people's misery than the schools, hospitals, and welfare offices. The latter, therefore, become the foci of attack, and the movements develop an ideology to counter the Progressive ideology which supports these institutions.[14]

Moreover, the more extreme leftist ideologies have been discredited in American politics even among low-income citizens. Hence, there is no clear option for low-income organizing on the ideological left.

ACORN's literature, public pronouncements and organizing practice have dealt with this dilemma in several ways: (1) ACORN describes itself as "populist"; (2) it has taken a consistent

34

anti-corporate stance; and (3) it has eschewed formal ideology and promoted an "action as ideology" approach, especially in its internal communications. The combination of these three approaches creates confusion, but may provide some important insights for the use of ideology as an incentive in low-income organizing.

ACORN frequently refers to itself, on fliers and in the press, as "populist". The term, however, denotes little and connotes much. It has been associated with a wide variety of political views and politicians, as well as a major political movement of the late nineteenth century. Political scientists have rarely tried to use the term with any precision, associating it negatively with racism and anti-intellectualism[15] or positively with the practice of initiative and referendum and increased political participation generally.[16] Recent historical revision by Lawrence Goodwyn[17] has altered the view of the Populist Movement. He argues that the Populists were egalitarian anticapitalists, not the backward-looking racist romantics many historians have depicted.

Similarly, George McKenna argues that populism is a genuine ideology with a reasonable degree of complexity and an historic consistency. He attempts to document this with letters, speeches and platforms from American political history. McKenna distills six basic tenets of populistic ideology: (1) lack of class consciousness; (2) the assumption of consensus among "the people"; (3) strong patriotism; (4) the belief that wealth should belong to all Americans; (5) a fear of bigness -- corporate or governmental; and (6) mistrust of intellectual elites. ACORN's rhetoric and strategy bear striking similarities to populism.

ACORN's avowed aim is to organize the lower seventy percent on the income ladder. ACORN rhetoric always refers to "the people", and avoids identifying race, gender, class, region, or other divisions among Americans. ACORN operates on the assumption that American society is divided between "low- and moderate-income people," or "the people," and the "fatcats" or "the few." However, ACORN does not expound theories of class struggle; it keeps the analysis at the level of "the people" struggling to be heard or the "majority" trying to "take control of the government." Like the Populists, ACORN maintains that the struggle is between "the many" and "the few."

ACORN operates on the premise that "the people" generally agree on "what is right and wrong, fair and foul, legitimate and crooked."[19] ACORN organizers argue that as long as ACORN deals

primarily with economic issues or building political power, low-
and moderate-income people will hold together.[20] ACORN's
People's Platform, for example, clearly avoids social issues such
as ERA and busing. As Gary Delgado argues, "[l]ike many populist
organizations ACORN ... opted to preserve class unity by
developing an anti-corporate political program that did not
directly address salient issues of race and sex."[21] This has
been an integral part of ACORN's organizing strategy from its
inception: to organize people around economic issues, target
government and corporations and avoid divisive social issues.

Patriotism has not been a salient issue in ACORN's history.
The only germane activities are ACORN protests of President
Reagan's increased military spending, and in some instances, the
nuclear freeze. However, there have been no Vietnams to divide
people who might otherwise unite, or to raise doubts about the
patriotism of ACORN as an organization.

ACORN's ideological approach to private property is similar
to McKenna's depiction of populism. ACORN expresses the idea
that "the land and commodities of America belong not to some but
to all of the American people" in both word and deed. The ACORN
People's Platform provides clear evidence of this belief in the
preamble; it demands "the best of our energy, land, and natural
resources for all people." The clearest expression of this
belief came from ACORN's "squatting" campaign. ACORN saw a
contradiction between a housing shortage on the one hand, and the
existence of thousands of vacant houses in ACORN neighborhoods on
the other. These houses had been abandoned by their owners,
frequently they had been taken by city and federal governments
for unpaid taxes, HUD mortgage foreclosures, or other reasons.
ACORN organized public rallies to break into and claim the houses
for low-income families in need of housing. Claiming no legal
grounds for their actions, ACORN instead justified and publicized
squatting on the moral grounds that people were "Taking What's
Ours!" Many squatters were evicted and arrested for trespassing,
but in Congressional hearings ACORN members expressed
determination to continue squatting despite police and official
action.[22] Hence, unused resources -- in this case, abandoned
houses -- have been claimed by ACORN to promote views on human
rights versus property rights.

McKenna's claim regarding populist fears of bigness is
somewhat muddled in ACORN. Delgado argues, for example, that the
People's Platform expresses "ambivalence between anti-corporate
populism and the social-democratic state."[23] While a great
deal of the platform is directed at control of corporate abuses,

and the difficulty of controlling big government, some of the proposals would require massive bureaucracies and tremendous budget outlays that have historically led to unresponsiveness to and abuse of low-income citizens. The demand for federal programs to build a million units of housing per year contradicts both an organizing strategy which dictates extreme localism and human scale, and the association bylaws which include an explicit goal of maintaining organizational democracy. Thus, ACORN appears ambivalent about the most desirable size of institutions; it struggles against large corporations and government bureaucracies, but at times is attracted to large government programs.

ACORN has had little to say about intellectual elites, the last tenet of populism that McKenna cites. ACORN chapters have frequently been involved in public education affairs, including promoting legislation for free textbooks in Arkansas and running and supporting candidates to school boards. However, there have been no issues or statements akin to William Jennings Bryant's behavior at the Scopes Trial or George Wallace's attacks on "intellectual snobs."[24]

Anti-Ideology in _ACORN_. ACORN's internal approach to ideology and action is quite unusual for an apparently leftist organization. ACORN's avowed reasons for being anti-ideological are (1) the goal of redistributing power is adequate inspiration and direction, (2) political understanding is best gained by experience rather than study, and (3) given the complexity of society, it is impossible to predict the best means of redistributing power in every policy area.

Kest and Rathke argue that specific issues and policy stands are not the essence of ACORN's activities. Rather, they contend, "[b]ehind the organization's concern with these issues is a basic understanding that all these issues are mere manifestations of a much more fundamental issues: the distribution of power in the country."[25] Hence, this is the single concern that the organizers of ACORN address.

ACORN also claims that a well-developed ideology is not useful for community organizing because political knowledge cannot be imparted without a solid base of participatory involvement. Indeed, one of the most important reasons for actively involving members is to provide them with a good understanding of the political system and the alleged maldistribution of power. ACORN aims to put low- and moderate-income people in situations where their reasonable demands are resisted or rejected. In this way, they will learn what to expect from politicians and corporate representatives. Fainstein and Fainstein observed this same process at work in several urban political movements they studied.[26] Having experienced first-hand the maldistribution of power, ACORN participants are then likely to see that the connections between their immediate issue and other issues revolve around the distribution of power.

Finally, the ACORN approach assumes that the organization should only make policy stances on issues in which it is actively involved. ACORN strategists argue that it is unwise to make claims regarding a policy area which does not directly affect the organization's members. Further, it makes no sense to take a position without being willing and able to act on it. Thus, until the group is in a position of some power and has organized constituents around an issue, there is no benefit and possibly some danger in taking a position on it.

Rathke claims that "[a]n organization like ACORN doesn't develop an ideology until it finishes growing, until it has some power to exercise ... I'm confident that that process produces the best of all philosophies and ideologies."[27] When the organization's precepts are kept simple, action serves educational functions and the group only takes issue stances on policy matters in which it is active. This assures that the organization's needs can be met, and also that it will not be encumbered with ideological baggage that can lead to the kinds of goal displacement that Moe describes.

Thus, ACORN's anti-ideological approach stems from several concerns regarding the low- and moderate-income constituency: (1) power in American life is maldistributed; (2) knowledge comes from power; and (3) action is the most effective means of learning and expressing political values. This level of abstraction and analysis appears to provide sufficient direction to ACORN organizers and members without painting them into the corner of goal displacement and organizer dominance. The combination of the vague popular understanding of populism and fear of the organizers' abuse of ideology warrants describing ACORN as "anti-ideological."

Anti-corporatism in ACORN. The third dimension of ACORN's purposive incentives is a crude anti-corporatism. Kest and Rathke argue that the most important fact about high utility rates is that "in reality rather than rhetoric a bunch of corporate directors and New York bankers have the power to unilaterally make decisions that affect the lives of ACORN members."[28] This claim that economic power is undemocratic and should be redressed by political action permeates all of ACORN's activism and rhetoric. ACORN chapters have fought corporations over toxic waste disposal, utility rates, plant sitings, tax structures and abatements, banking and investment practices, and many other issues. The preamble to the ACORN People's Platform specifies a subordinate rather than dominant role for corporations in American society: "Corporations shall have their role: producing jobs, providing products, paying taxes. No more. No less. They shall obey our wishes, respond to our needs, serve our communities."

In sum, ACORN's approach to ideology is a form of praxis, where action informs thought. This is augmented by the vague yet appealing principles of populism, the "perennial" protest ideology of American politics, and a crude form of anti-corporatism. ACORN's history, its literature and the comments of observers substantiate the nature of ACORN's ideology and suggest that it is effective in overcoming some of the difficulties in using ideology as a purposive incentive for low- and moderate-income Americans.

The Members' Contribution

ACORN organizers make it clear that prospective members must contribute substantially to the organization for it to succeed. One of the major goals of the organizers in the organizing drive is to collect dues before the first meeting. This alone makes the exchange relationship clear: members must provide the means by which the organization survives. ACORN uses the "membership organization" principle. Members and prospective members are thus initiated into the organization with a clear message that their role in the organization is contributory and not passive.

One of the clearest assertions of members' financial role in ACORN stems from the organizational goal of financial self-sufficiency. The "ACORN Members' Handbook" states

> ACORN has always been committed to the principle of financial self-sufficiency and we've made great strides toward that goal. The principle is important because only an organization that raises and controls its own funds can be truly independent. Because ACORN members pay the organization's way, we call the shots.[29]

39

Hence, despite ACORN's lower income constituency, the organization requires its members to contribute dues regularly and with great emphasis.

ACORN organizers are also advised to persuade members to contribute as much time as possible to the organization. This begins with the exhortation to assist in the large task of doorknocking the entire neighborhood in the organizing drive. The Organizing Model quite bluntly sets the agenda for Organizing Committee meetings: "Doorknocking: Get agreements on when, not if."[30] The organizers are also trained to delegate as many of the group's other duties as possible, including phoning, taking parts of the meeting agendas, distributing fliers, and fundraising. Moreover, ACORN actions are designed to involve as many people as possible. Thus, members are expected to give a great deal of time and commitment. The Organizing Model is quite explicit about the nature of the exchange relationship:

> Contract: Make clear [w]hat they can expect from ACORN (services, research, assistance, contacts, political power, literatures [sic], etc.), and what ACORN expects of the group (dues, affiliation, news distribution, etc.).[31]

Organizational Structure

ACORN's organizational structure can be described by its organizational groupings, the three roles of participants in the organization, and the committee and governing structures above the local level. All of these features were designed to contribute to the success of the organization by expressing its values and filling constituent needs.

ACORN's basic component is the neighborhood organization. One cannot be a member of ACORN unless one contributes dues and participates in one's neighborhood group. The neighborhood structure is intended to provide a physical association for the membership, i.e., the organization represents a geographical entity with clearly defined boundaries. Besides providing members with territorial allegiances, geographical basing provides a sense of permanence, according to Kest and Rathke:

> To its members, the organization, rather than just whatever issue is being worked on at that time, is of number one importance. The point is that in order to address the fundamental

> questions of power, low- and moderate-income
> citizens must be organized; in other words, be
> committed to a permanent organization that,
> over the long run, will attack the
> maldistribution of power in every way it
> can.[32]

This sense of permanence provides a concrete representation of
the necessarily long-term mission.

The local nature of the organization also makes the
experience of membership personal and tangible. Upper-income
Americans frequently participate in politics by writing checks to
distant post office boxes and following the organization in the
papers and monthly newsletters. Lower income citizens, however,
respond better to visible, tangible, and local organizations.
The members are able to meet face-to-face with leaders and can
personalize the organization rather than experience it only
abstractly.

Historically, lower-income people have seen organizations
come and go and the resulting mistrust of organizational
solutions to their problems creates the need to overcome
constituents' skepticism. This is done by keeping the local
groups close to the members, both geographically and temporally.
The local groups meet monthly. They constantly work in issues
within both the neighborhood and the larger community, along with
other local groups. This keeps the organization constantly in
view and maintains enough momentum to keep members motivated.

The local groups consist of approximately 100-200 members
who hold membership cards and pay dues. They are, for the most
part, the people in the neighborhood who joined during the
organizing drive or at the first meeting. Active participants
number far fewer than the entire membership. Active members are
generally the officers and a loyal cadre, usually around a dozen
people in all. They attend meetings regularly, respond to
requests to assist in distributing fliers and making calls, and
participate in actions. Moreover, they serve on larger,
community-wide committees such as the ACORN Political Action
Committees. The disparity between active and inactive members is
calculated into the organizing strategy, as expressed in the
Organizing Model:

> Attendance: The majority of first meetings are
> the biggest meetings that groups will ever
> have, depending on the quality of the issues.

> Build a core which you can depend on for
> consistency in the group in both size and
> quality. This is a natural organizational
> event. You must convince the groups, though,
> that they never have enough people to be
> satisfied, but don't allow numbers to depress
> their activity or stability.[33]

Thus, the reality -- a small core of activists -- is accounted
for in the organizing strategy, yet an ideal is established that
prods the activists to greater efforts to expand their numbers.
The activities of this cadre, meanwhile, represent the tangible
organizational solution to neighborhood political problems.

Participant Roles

The three roles in ACORN are member, leader, and organizer.
They are clearly defined in the organizing strategy and are
essential to understanding the nature of the organization.
Briefly, members pay dues and participate in the organization.
Leaders are formally elected or appointed to interim posts.
Organizers are paid, professional participants who are not
indigenous to the neighborhood, and rarely come from the
constituency.

Members are formally designated by being current on their
dues and possessing membership cards. As stated above, members
must reside in an ACORN neighborhood. They receive ACORN
publications and have access to the ACORN organizers and
services.

Leaders come from the membership, i.e., they are residents
of the neighborhood who have agreed to serve in positions in the
local group. Occasionally, interim officers are appointed when
circumstances require it, such as the sudden departure of a
current officer. Leaders are required to operate the group:
chairing meetings, leading actions, and conferring with
organizers on the organization's operations. Offices in a
typical neighborhood are chair, co-chair, secretary and
treasurer. While the roles are not tightly defined, generally
the chair and the co-chair provide executive leadership, the
secretary fulfills communications functions, and the treasurer
maintains dues records and keeps the books.

As in any voluntary organization, organizers are the only
paid participants in ACORN. They are demographically quite
different from the members and leaders and serve at the pleasure

of the Head Organizer. Organizers are almost all well-educated, white, middle- and upper-income young people. ACORN recruits them most frequently from Eastern colleges and universities, but they are then assigned to posts anywhere in the twenty-six ACORN states or the District of Columbia. Thus, there is some built-in distance between the members and the leaders, and the organizers -- social, economic, geographical, educational, and frequently racial. In addition, the organizers' allegiance is to the organization at large while the members tend to perceive the organization mostly within their neighborhoods. Finally, the organizers see themselves as professionals applying skills and ethical standards, while the constituents are mainly concerned with issues and power.

Although the ACORN model is built on member control and participation, the nature of the organizers tends to mitigate against this approach. While the organizers are trained and encouraged to delegate as many of their functions as possible, they tend to do as much of the work as they can. The organizers, many of them high achievers, feel the responsibility of their jobs rather heavily and become uncomfortable when others are doing the job for them. Structurally, the role of the organizer counterposed against the constituency is a source of conflict within the ACORN organizing strategy.

Regional Structure

The two main regional structures are the Executive Board and the ACORN Political Action Committee (APAC). They manage the citywide (or, in the case of rural areas, countywide) executive and electoral activities of ACORN, respectively. The Executive Committee, which consists of the neighborhood chairs, meets monthly to make the broader regional decisions. The Head Organizer of the area reports to the Executive Committee and confers with it on issues, strategies, and financial affairs.

The APAC conducts the electoral activities of the regional group by analyzing campaigns, interviewing candidates -- if any -- to support, and coordinate the electoral efforts of the regional ACORN group. Both of these bodies offer members and leaders opportunities to contribute, control, and participate in the larger workings of ACORN. Like any board of directors or political action group, they exercise as much control as they see fit and oversee staff (organizers) as closely as they feel is necessary. There is nothing absolute about their functioning. This is in keeping with standard practices in voluntary organizations of any kind.

POLITICAL ORGANIZING IN GRASSROOTS POLITICS

This chapter has described the organizing strategy of the ACORN model. The strategy is clearly adapted to ACORN's constituency and goals. Moreover, it is clear that the decisions that go into it are conscious and goal-directed. Thus, the organizing strategy can provide insights into the model ACORN applies in organizing its constituency for political power. The chapters that follow will examine the experiences and insights of Boston ACORN participants through interviews, in order to determine the impact of the organizing strategy on its participants.

Consistent with the notion of the organizer/entrepreneur as the rational (and, historically speaking, actual) progenitor of the political organization, we will first look at the perceptions of the professional organizers. The interviews in Chapter 5 will attempt to establish their intentions and determine what effects they wish to create among their targeted constituents. Once this is established, interviews with the members and leaders (the constituents) will provide insights into their effectiveness and their perceptions of the organization and the organizing strategy.

Notes to Chapter III

[1] Wade Rathke, quoted in Andrew Kopkind, "ACORN Calling: Door-to-Door Organizing in Arkansas," Working Papers 3, no. 3 (Summer, 1975), p. 14.

[2] Gary Delgado, "Organizing the Movement," Diss. Univ. of California, Berkeley School of Social Work, 1984, p. 50.

[3] Steven Kest and Wade Rathke, "ACORN: An Overview," in Community Organizing Handbook #2 (New Orleans: The Institute for Social Justice, 1979), p. 3.

[4] Delgado, p. 51.

[5] "ACORN Community Organizing Model," (mimeographed, n.d.), p. 1.

[6] Kest and Rathke, p. 4.

[7] Ibid.

[8] Ibid., p. 7.

[9] Gary Delgado, Organizing the Movement (Philadelphia:

Temple Univ. Press, 1986), p. 187.

[10]"ACORN Community Organizing Model," p. 5.

[11]Ibid., p. 9.

[12]Ibid., p. 11.

[13]Ibid., p. 6.

[14]Norman I. Fainstein and Susan S. Fainstein, Urban Political Movements (Englewood Cliffs, N.J.: Prentice-Hall, Inc., 1974), p. 56.

[15]Robert Hofstadter, Anti-Intellectualism in American Life (New York: Alfred A. Knopf, 1963).

[16]Robert Dahl, A Preface to Democratic Theory (New Haven: Yale Univ. Press, 1965), pp. 34-62.

[17]Lawrence Goodwyn, The Populist Moment (New York: Oxford Univ. Press, 1978), pp. 334-342. He clarifies the use of the term "populism" in history and social science.

[18]George McKenna, American Populism (New York: G.P. Putnam's Sons, 1974).

[19]Ibid., p. xiii.

[20]Kest and Rathke, p. 4.

[21]Delgado, diss., p. 64.

[22]Hearings before the House Subcommittee on Housing and Community Development of the Committee on Banking, Finance, and Urban Affairs, 24 June, 1982, author in attendance.

[23]Delgado, Ibid.

[24]George Wallace quoted in McKenna, p. 222.

[25]Kest and Rathke, Ibid.

[26]Fainstein and Fainstein, pp. 182-183.

[27]Wade Rathke quoted in Martin Kirby, "A Citizen Action Force That Really Works," Southern Voices, 10 no. 2 (May/June,

1974), n.p.

[28]Kest and Rathke, Ibid.

[29]"ACORN Members' Handbook" (mimeographed, n.d.), p. 5.

[30]"ACORN Community Organizing Model," p. 10.

[31]Ibid.

[32]Kest and Rathke, p. 5.

[33]"ACORN Community Organizing Model," p. 19.

C H A P T E R   I V

THE ORGANIZERS

Interviews with ACORN organizers were designed to ascertain their perceptions of their roles and the impact of their activities. Clearly, their role as the professional staff and entrepreneurs of the organizing strategy is critical to an understanding of ACORN; they "sell" membership and participation in ACORN in return for benefits they claim they can supply. The responses of the organizers will be discussed under four broad headings: (1) their impressions of the nature of ACORN organizing; (2) their impressions of the benefits members derive from ACORN; (3) their perceptions of the decision making process; and (4) problems they encounter in their work.

ACORN organizers consider themselves professionals -- political activists who possess practical and ethical standards of performance -- and I approached them as such.

Organizers' Incentives

The organizers' perceptions of the experience of ACORN organizing derive from their reasons for becoming ACORN organizers, the satisfactions they receive from their work, and their experience with ACORN organizing. Their impetus to "hire on" appears to be either ideological or social. The ideological attraction of ACORN stems from its commitment to social change and social justice for low- and moderate-income people. The organizers themselves were all oriented to left-wing political activities prior to becoming ACORN organizers. For example, here are three organizers:

> I was a radical in college and involved in a student group there. I'd planned to work for social change some way after I got out of school. I wanted to go into the trade union movement but I ... didn't know how to do that ... I found out about ACORN ... and sent in an application.

> I'd always been interested in progressive stuff

47

> ... I'd done a fair amount of work for a couple
> of years out of college with some peace and
> social justice organizations, working on
> international and foreign relations, things
> like that, so, I'd gotten fairly frustrated
> with, number one, there were never any concrete
> results, and number two, it really did seem we
> were talking to the same people. So ACORN is a
> real change of pace.
>
> I had been involved in other things, like peace
> stuff, and that just didn't seem to be valid
> and it seemed to be a shell game. I became
> convinced very quickly that the only way to do
> something about the arms race was to radically
> restructure the society that implied the arms
> race. And any of the peace organizations that
> are around now aren't in the least bit
> interested in changing anything. That was the
> conclusion that I arrived at and ACORN seemed
> to be the organization that was interested in
> changing some very basic things in American
> society, trying to change the way people think
> about themselves and their environment. So
> that's why I began working for ACORN.

It is notable, too, that this group, while not a valid sample of
ACORN organizers nationally, emphasized foreign policy issues as
the focus of their pre-ACORN activism.

The other major factor in their decisions to become ACORN
organizers was the opportunity to explore a part of American
society that was new to them. As a grassroots organization that
works directly in the neighborhoods, ACORN puts its organizers in
frequent direct contact with low-income minority people within
their communities. Hence, one organizer responded that he was
greatly motivated to become an ACORN organizer by his desire to
learn about the ACORN constituency; his curiosity was first
aroused by his study of social anthropology in college. For the
ideologue, the opportunity to work directly with low- and
moderate-income people also provides a test of ideological
assumptions.

For the most part, the organizers' experiences either met or
exceeded their expectations:

> Very much so and very much better. I couldn't

imagine myself, after working on disarmament,
getting terribly excited about vacant lots and
stop signs and all. But it obviously turned
out to be a lot more exciting than I expected
it to be.

It's a down-to-earth, seriously organized
group. I didn't expect it to be so tight and
well run. In terms of other organizations I've
been involved in, being able to lay out a plan
and go through with it, being able to make
plans for a year or more and being able to
respond in a real way to things that are
happening in the community and the country.

In recruiting new organizers -- usually, college-educated,
white, middle-class people like themselves -- the organizers
voice the same themes. They try simultaneously to make the
experience of ACORN organizing attractive and to interpret the
experience for someone relatively unfamiliar with it.

What I try to do ... is to try to deal with
them the same way I deal with members. Before
I launch into my song and dance, I listen to
them to see what interests them, what motivates
them politically. I talk a lot about action.
I talk a lot about the transformation that you
can see happening in leaders and in members who
never thought of themselves as ever being
anything but a domestic worker. They get on TV
two weeks after they join ACORN, yelling at the
mayor ... and everybody on the block pats them
on the back, and it really does change the way
people look at themselves.

I also spend a good deal of time trying to
differentiate between ACORN and other groups.
I know when I was in college, to me, I had
heard about ACORN and ACORN was like the
Mobilization for Survival, like all those
left-center political groups. I didn't really
understand what made ACORN different.

I think the contact with people in the
neighborhood is a major factor in new
organizers. Basically, try to make people feel
comfortable on the job. You can get people to

give you the political rap about anything, but
they won't be willing to do the work.

These themes -- social justice, organizational
effectiveness, and social contact with the constituents --
prevail in the discussion of the experience. They also dominate
the responses to questions about the kinds of satisfaction
organizers have received, ACORN's national goals, and their
perception of ACORN's success.

The pursuit of social justice remains a primary motivation
of organizers after their decision to join and after they have
been on the staff long enough for the novelty to wear off:

> What I get out of it is the sense that I'm part
> of a movement [that] ... in the end will lead
> to a revolution and will, in time, increase the
> power of working people. To overcome the
> system. Being involved in that is what I want
> to be right now and what I want to do. And in
> a lot of day-to-day stuff in ACORN you don't
> really see that very much, but things like
> Dallas, or when you have a good action against
> ... one of the city officials or housing
> officials, you can really see clearly what the
> people can do, how people get a sense of their
> power as a group.

What keeps the job satisfying, according to the organizers, is
the experience and assurance of success in pursuit of social
justice. This point is particularly critical when the organizers
compare ACORN relative to other, less successful groups with the
same goals, as well as when they consider the relatively
powerless status of their constituency:

> During the 70s and 80s, no other left-wing
> organization has really survived and prospered
> in any real sense like ACORN has ... and
> they've been around for fourteen years [sic].
> As far as an independent, self-financing
> organization, I don't know any other
> organization in the country that does that ...
> apart from unions or somebody that gets serious
> money from foundations ... Obviously, I think
> we're doing much better than other
> organizations, or I wouldn't stick with it. I
> think we are having an effect, particularly in

the political arena. Jesse Jackson's folks --
the way they courted our participation in a
number of states was pretty amazing, and sort
of gratifying. It's gratifying that other
people are beginning to recognize the skills
and power that we do have. Locally, Mel King,
we busted our butts for him last fall, and in
many ways it's paid off for us. He's going to
raise $500 for APAC this year. He's writing a
letter for us that says ACORN helped me in my
campaign, you should give them money, going out
to the people in his campaign as well as to
other lefties around town, and things like that
...

In the last year and a half ... I've almost had
to define "success" as survival. We went
through a couple of really bad years, really
hard years. And we came through them okay,
with a strong organization and having won some
victories along the way. It speaks to some
internal strength that we did survive the last
couple of years. A lot of organizations
didn't. A lot of people went under or stopped
organizing because of something else. And
we're moving in broader directions ... In most
cities that I know close up, it isn't at the
expense of the neighborhood base. We can still
call ourselves, and mean it, "grassroots."

Clearly, the organizers feel that the goal of social justice is
not sufficient to keep them involved; success is also necessary.
But they perceive success as rare among such organizations.

Finally, social interactions are an effective motivation for
staying on the job. For example:

It's in contact with a new segment of the
population. Which is basically the people we
deal with ... mostly black ... it's a really
now exposure to me, so I enjoy it. I think the
fact of working with some of the people I work
with is one of the best parts of the job ...

On a personal level, I just love our members,
they're just tremendous people. At this stage
of the ballgame, one of the things that keeps

me going is personal connections on the staff.
I have a tremendous respect for our staff.
Over the last several months I've been
traveling around and my assumption has always
been that all these people whose names I'd read
on the charts were, in fact, (a) wonderful
people, and (b) good organizers. It's been
confirmed time and time again over the last six
to eight months.

The organizers reported satisfaction from getting to know a new
segment of the population, individuals among that segment, and
their fellow ACORN staff. Those incentives, coupled with the
ideological goals, comprise the bulk of the reasons organizers
work with ACORN. None cited any other commonly used incentives
such as income, flexible work hours, working conditions, fringe
benefits, and so on.

The Organizer Role

The interviewees also centered on the relationships they
developed in the course of the organizing work. While some of
their experiences provide insight into the organizer's role in
ACORN, others reflect the nature of the work.

It is important to recognize the context of the organizers'
responses. Their work for ACORN is usually their first full-time
employment after graduation from college. All have some
experience as political activists in other organizations. But,
clearly, their venture from middle-class backgrounds into low-
and moderate-income neighborhoods can be profoundly different.
Moreover, the organizing profession is different from other
occupations in many ways.

The organizers sounded two clear themes: (1) they "inject"
themselves into peoples' lives, neighborhoods, and political
relationships, and (2) they must change peoples' lives in order
to succeed. Thus, the organizers believe they occupy a somewhat
unusual position in society.

One of the essential roles of ACORN organizers is to knock
on peoples' doors and promote membership:

Part of the reason we have the ability to go
door-to-door to recruit people that other
organizations don't is because we have
full-time professional organizers. A group can

> maintain itself at some level without an
> organizing staff, but there's always some
> amount of attrition, and unless there's some
> constant recruitment of new members, it's just
> a matter of time before the group kind of dies,
> or doesn't move forward.

At the same time, the experience is at first somewhat alien to
the organizers.

> The organizing part of it is strange. Knocking
> for three hours at strange doors, asking to
> come in the door, we talk with them, and for me
> it's something I've never done before.

> Just by going door-knocking every day, you're
> challenging peoples' interests of privacy and
> property, and that varies from person to person
> ... That may see very trivial, but it has
> implications for much larger schemes of
> thinking.

That same sense of privacy appeared to constrain some organizers'
behavior:

> Not long ago, one of our newer staff members
> expressed some hesitation about doing second
> and third visits to people on a drive because
> he felt like it would be kind of "hounding" the
> members. My experience has always been just
> the reverse. We always hear that the members
> don't hear from us enough; I've seen that
> happen.

A successful ACORN organizer must intrude beyond generally
acceptable levels of privacy in order to reach the constituents,
and not all organizers are entirely comfortable with this.

Once the organizers have entered their constituents' lives,
they work to change ideas about their neighborhoods and political
relationships. According to ACORN organizers, however, members'
thinking will not change by persuasion or lecturing. One
organizer reported that "what makes ACORN sometimes so
frustrating is that its structural ideas are so radically
different from the mainstream structure of ideas in the world
today." ACORN organizers believe experience is the only
effective means of imparting ACORN's "structural ideas" on

authority, social justice, the rights of low-income people, and other fundamental political concepts.

I asked one organizer if ACORN is able to educate its members in political matters:

> I think it's incredibly true for people who get involved. Both in terms of the resources available to the communities, more though, in terms of how the bureaucracy functions, how the government functions, who's who in politics, who's who in the power structure. I think it really breaks down a lot of peoples' notions of what seems it means to be in a position of authority. It helps them realize that the heads of all these agencies and all our targets are real people and they're really screwing up. It's been a real eye-opener for a lot of our members who are active ... they'll get involved, thinking all you have to do is write a letter to your councilman and you'll get this pothole repaired. Then people get active and realize that, no, people in City Hall have their own set of priorities and it's based on a whole different set of things. You need to influence that set of priorities.

From the organizer's viewpoint, then, "education" involves more than imparting information to members. Members must change their attitudes toward and their way of dealing with authority. Indeed, both to motivate members' activism and to overcome resistance, the organizing process itself teaches many of the same skills that ACORN's opponents use to block change:

> I was sort of disappointed to realize that people who work for ACORN don't think very differently from people who work for New York law firms. They don't think very differently from Madison Avenue advertising people. The strategies that we use are just as high-powered as any of the oppositions'. But on the other hand, if that's the way the American system works, we have to beat people at their own game ...
>
> They don't want thirty angry people showing up at their office with signs and chanting. It's

sort of like winning through intimidation. I
can think of one case. I had a two-week plan
around getting an enormous trench filled in.
All it took was one phone call. Someone called
and said they were from ACORN and they wanted
action now or we'd take some action, and it was
done that morning.

In order to carry out their mission as organizers, therefore, the
interviewees reported that they have to invade peoples' privacy,
pressure them to attend ACORN activities, and then apply strong
pressure to achieve goals that are not widely shared -- or even
understood -- by the majority of people in American society.

Membership Incentives

ACORN organizing is built around the incentives used to
persuade its constituents to join and participate. Organizers'
self-perceptions are critical to understanding these incentives.

The organizers see three factors in the members' decision to
join ACORN: self-interest, anger, and ACORN's organizational
identity. But self-interest is the organizers' bread-and-butter
when they are appealing for new members:

People join around very specific issues on
their streets and in their neighborhoods.
Something they feel very immediately. The
majority of our members join ... after an
organizer has knocked on their door and the
conversation is about the vacant lots on their
block or the school down the street. Housing
may be the number one issue, next to, maybe,
crime, that comes up on the doors. I think
initially people join out of some level of
self-interest on a specific issue.

We're concerned about these things in the
neighborhood ... basically the common
denominator, things that almost anybody in the
neighborhood, if they have any kind of desire
to improve the situation, will be upset about
... potholes, abandoned houses ... or if I work
in a tenants' group, the conditions of the
apartments ... that's what people really relate
to ...

> The obvious is the feeling that community
> improvements can be achieved. Whether they be
> small, whether they be big. I guess that's the
> most important one ...

The way self-interest operates in neighborhood organizing,
however, sometimes creates a dynamic that expands the benefits
beyond the individual and into the larger community:

> Some people, a person in my group is working
> really hard for a park which she would never
> use because she lives so far away from it. But
> she spends so much energy on it, it's crazy. I
> feel really strange about it. I think it's
> great. She tells me she wants to see something
> done. I think it's a commitment towards the
> community which she really likes ... and it's a
> commitment towards other members of the group
> that she enjoys that lives close to her.

Self-interest, then, is the mainstay of membership incentives.
But since ACORN organizes specific geographical areas,
self-interest can, at times, expand to include issues that are
somewhat removed from the specific individual.

One organizer took the notion of self-interest and
identification with one's neighborhood a step further, suggesting
that some members join out of a desire to support an organization
to represent the community:

> ... just to participate in being part of some
> organization within the community, the notion
> that the community has to be more unified and
> to participate in it. Some are really oriented
> toward the goals and some like the idea that
> there's a community group to belong to.

Hence, the notion that the organization needs support can
persuade some prospective members to join. Going a step farther,
another organizer stressed the value of using the strength of
numbers to persuade people to join ACORN:

> Sometimes, depending on where somebody is
> politically, I will talk about the general
> notion of having an effective organization,
> touch on a wide range of issues but usually
> just a real specific pitch emphasizing the idea

56

> that you and I can't do it. If you and I go
> down and complain 'bout getting a bus shelter,
> they're not going to listen to us. But I
> talked to six other people today, and they're
> concerned about it too ... We've got two
> hundred members in this group, don't you think
> even if half that many went downtown they'd get
> something done?

Effectiveness is thus important not only for organizers, but for
prospective members.

Finally, anger is important in the organizers' calculations
for appealing to prospective members. The organizers claim that
many of their constituents are people who have been frustrated
because their needs have been ignored for so long:

> People are attracted to ACORN because ... we do
> a lot of actions, we make a lot of noise, we
> get some stuff done, in terms of getting
> improvements in the neighborhood, different
> aspects of peoples' lives that before they
> didn't know they had any control over. People
> who are fed up with it and feel that if they
> band together they can get something done join
> ACORN because they see that it helps.

One organizer noted that the severe problems in many
neighborhoods effectively provoke anger as a stimulus to join:

> I ask very, very general questions and I use
> words like "change," "neighborhood," "What do
> you want?" "What do you think?" and sometimes
> people can't think of anything off the top of
> their head, so you toss off a couple of
> specifics. That can get people oiled up. They
> don't like the fact that there's a playground
> around the corner from them that's filled with
> drunks. You can get them steamed up about
> that. The ACORN model depends on playing on
> peoples' anger to get them to join, to get them
> to say what they already know ... and
> capitalizing on that to get them into the
> organization.

Part of the organizer's tool kit for recruiting new members,
therefore, is their constituents' anger over the condition of

their neighborhood or its lack of government services.

Although organizers argue that some members stay involved with ACORN for the continued supply of tangible rewards, they believe most ACORN members stay in the organization because of commitment to the organization and some intangible incentives. Clearly, however, the tangible incentives are not sufficient to maintain the organization:

> People often join for one very, very narrow reason, streetlights on their block, and then after they get them in the organization, they do work on other things. They see other reasons for having an organization like that.

> I think people stay involved over time because ... they develop ... a sense of what can be achieved through organizing. And then there's definitely a core of people ..., especially some of the leaders, who stay active out of a commitment to the notion of organizing. It definitely goes beyond the issues.

> Eventually, people go beyond an understanding of the group as just a neighborhood group but also a political force in the country. I think people get a sense of that after they've been involved in the organization for a while.

The organizers claim that the organization itself becomes the focus of the members' energies and the force that keeps them involved.

The organizers offered several explanations of why people become so committed to ACORN as an organization. The sum of these explanations seems to be a combination of qualities of ACORN and its committed members:

> I think that the general excitement of the group keeps people involved. Members like actions, they like to come to well-run meetings ... that do follow an agenda and get things accomplished. I'd say those two things, more than anything else. And a lot of our members, they just like the notion of fighting City Hall.

My experience has been ... that people who come
to three or more meetings or actions ... that's
the one objective determining factor. The
experience is somewhat addictive. I would say
that people who are willing to work, also,
that's a determining factor ... who aren't
incredibly busy or ... lazy. Again, people who
get out there and doorknock their block with an
organizer, who make phone calls for meetings
and all that kind of stuff, I think it sets up
a sort of dynamic in their head where it's very
difficult for them to live with the
inconsistency of investing all this time and
energy and then not coming out for the meetings
or actions themselves ... People who <u>stay</u>
involved are people who have a little bit of
time on their hands, are genuinely concerned
about their neighborhoods and neighborhood
issues, and we've gotten to come out two or
three times.

I think that what enhances peoples' commitment
is just that they do something that changes
their way of thinking, they participate in some
kind of action where the action gets something
accomplished or at least they scare a person
that they see has been pushing them around for
a long time or ignoring them. Or if you have a
big meeting and you have a new person who
chairs it or takes a big part of the agenda.
That's the sort of thing that enhances their
commitment or it sort of divides ...; some
people will do that and feel really good about
it ... other people won't be able to handle it.

In essence, the organizers believe that when the right kind of
people are exposed to ACORN they will develop commitment to the
organization. Note the features of ACORN activism that they
claim will create this effect for the members: excitement,
effectiveness in fighting City Hall, addiction, consistency of
action and thought, vented anger, and the opportunity to assume
responsibility. Because they believe the ACORN experience
effectively creates the desire for more, the organizers strongly
affirm that persistence is the key to ACORN's success:

It would <u>have</u> to be ACORN's organizational
persistence. They don't let go of people.

> People who have achieved a goal of theirs and
> don't come out to meetings for a while but
> they're on your list and you call them anyway.
> And then, once in a while something comes up
> and they do come out. I think what keeps
> people in is that once ACORN has its grip on
> someone, they don't let go.

Finally, one of the organizers expressed the belief that
ACORN taps low-income people's understanding that they should
belong to organizations like ACORN:

> Just the fact that they're joining an
> organization shows some kind of knowledge that
> poor people, wherever they are, have to get
> together to get organized. There's already
> that germ of consciousness about how poor
> people have the same problems everywhere and
> got to get together. I think getting involved
> in the organization deepens their understanding
> of that.

He claims that once this understanding is actualized through
participating, it becomes the source of continuing commitment to
the organization.

Several organizers suggested that purposive incentives also
promote members' participation in ACORN. One organizer suggested
that that was the only way the organization could survive:

> What gets them in is a more narrow view, what
> keeps them in is a broader view ... [K]eeping
> members involved is so difficult because if you
> look at it, we either fight that specific issue
> that they're concerned about and win, they'll
> go home and not come out again. If we fight on
> an issue and lose, ... they'll probably have
> even more reason not to stay involved in the
> group, or we don't tackle the issue at all.
> Again, if that's why you joined, they won't be
> inclined to stay involved, so the pressures or
> forces that keep people from staying involved
> are pretty high.

By this logic, for ACORN to persist, it must recruit members
who respond to incentives that are not purely self-interested.
The organizers suggested that that was possible in several ways.

THE ORGANIZERS

First, one organizer argued that the members

> ... are sophisticated enough. You have to give
> them credit. Just because they aren't <u>saying</u>
> it doesn't mean they aren't thinking it. You
> just haven't asked them the right question, you
> haven't spoken to them at the right time ...

Another organizer argued that purposive incentives allow the
individual to feel personally rewarded for making a contribution
toward a public good:

> Probably the greatest selective incentive we
> provide is the <u>in</u>tangible one: people knowing
> that they're part of an organization that is
> fighting for a lot of important things. That's
> why press coverage is so important, so that our
> members that don't ever come out to meetings
> can ... see ACORN on TV fighting to get a
> traffic light at a dangerous intersection. It
> makes them feel really proud. I think <u>that's</u> a
> real selective benefit, because other than
> their church, there aren't that many
> organizations our members can feel like are
> good, positive, helpful organizations that they
> belong to. There are service organizations
> like Eastern Star, ... but I think it's a
> different feeling for most of our members.

> If we're defining that sense of "I'm involved
> in something important," ... as the major
> selective benefit, then certainly people who
> feel that more emphatically, people who have
> been defining themselves all their lives as
> being fighters, they definitely participate.
> That woman, ... all of her life, she's defined
> herself as somebody who stands up for the
> little guy and fights to change stuff, doesn't
> take "no" for an answer. And for that reason,
> ... she's out to <u>everything</u>.

Thus, members apparently derive benefits from believing they
contribute to the public good. Paradoxically, however, the same
organizer who argued for the effectiveness of selective purposive
incentives also argued that ACORN organizations must provide
tangible benefits in order to succeed:

Members say you gotta crawl before you can walk. So we do that in organizing. By working on tangible, winnable, immediate, specific kinds of issues. We don't knock on somebody's door and talk to them about ... socialized medicine. We deal with those issues that we know we can win and we can look at and point to. And when one of their neighbors say, "That guy who was at your house -- is he from ACORN? Did you join that group? Do they get anything done?" They can point to something.

Most people like to see something visible. Again, there are [those] ... who understand what the whole struggle is about and we can probably go a year without actually winning something concrete in her particular neighborhood. She won't necessarily be disappointed. But she's obviously the exception ... People who respond most to that sort of approach are people who have tried on their own ... The people who have, for example, called the ambulance and had the ambulance not show up for forty-five minutes and then they read that the ... city is going to triple the ambulance fee. They respond much better.

His argument makes two basic points: (1) the organization must keep working on tangible benefits in order to keep recruits; and (2) those who respond primarily to selective purposive incentives are really quite rare; they cannot be counted to constitute the entire organization.

The organizers, therefore, offered a wide variety of comments on the kinds of incentives that they offer to their constituents in return for joining and participating in an ACORN group. The incentive that plays the biggest role, both in recruitment and maintenance, is the specific tangible benefit that satisfies constituents' self-interests. The organizers claimed that it is not only a necessary component of the recruitment process, but also actually quite significant in maintaining the ACORN group. The other three incentives that they felt were important in their efforts to create and maintain ACORN groups were anger, the organization itself, and purposive incentives. By their account, they are able to use all of these resources to persuade their constituents to participate in ACORN.

THE ORGANIZERS

Organizational Goals

The interview also elicited organizer responses about the kinds of goals ACORN could pursue, given the nature of its constituency. Their responses reflected their relationship to the ACORN members as professional organizers, and their use of issues as organizing tools. This discussion will deal with the organizers' perception of: (1) how broad ACORN's goals can be; (2) what limits exist and why; and (3) how flexible the members are.

The two most experienced organizers had a great deal to say about the value of expanding the issue agenda. At the same time they recognized that as a difficult task:

> It should be broader ... in that -- we'll probably always be able to say this, or I'll be able to say this -- again, because of the intense day-to-day demands, ... when doing direct neighborhood organizing, I didn't spend nearly enough time talking with the leaders and members about the broader issues involved. I would talk to them about why it's important to work on this campaign or that campaign, and ... in a campaign against a landlord, I'd talk about a particular landlord and the injustices that we've got to fight to change, but not often enough did I spend time talking about the larger housing issue -- why landlords get by with this sort of thing. I sort of did with leaders but not enough with members. Part of our whole philosophy or outlook is that people don't learn those kinds of things from conversation, they learn them from actions.

Issue generation, or the process by which ACORN organizers raise and articulate issues that are both concrete and important to the constituents, poses the difficulty of translating what organizers see as worthwhile goals into campaigns the constituents will support:

> Often times, I think I have to work harder to get peoples' interest, or make people understand why this particular issue is very important even though their neighbors aren't knocking on their doors saying, "Hey, why aren't you guys out there doing voter

> registration?" So I think we have to work with
> some of those issues a little bit harder and we
> have to dig deeper into our membership and find
> the people who are motivated by those things.

His solution to this dilemma is ACORN's pursuit of many goals at
the same time:

> That's one of the benefits of being a
> multi-issue organization; people who are going
> to be coming to tonight's APAC meeting ... may
> not have come to neighborhood actions for four
> or five months. They're just not that
> concerned with potholes or whatever, but they
> do understand the importance of electoral
> politics.

The organizers see as their goal imparting their
understanding of political issues to the members through
political action on those issues. The potential for such a
broadened understanding is equal to the members' potential for
learning from experience, either in ACORN or -- as the following
statement indicates -- from daily life.

> ERA, that surprised me that's on there. It is
> a less concrete kind of issue among the issues
> on here. It doesn't surprise me in that most
> of the people that you talked to are women that
> are really struggling in their lives, but I
> wouldn't have thought there would've been as
> much of a consensus down the line on that.
> There's no question that the consensus comes
> out of peoples' experiences and where people
> agree, it's on issues that they're dealing with
> every day.

One goal of ACORN organizing, therefore, is to reconcile the
organizers' political views with the daily lives of their
constituents by changing the latters' lives to include political
activism:

> The way a lot of these things can become
> reality is only by doing the kind of work that
> we do. I think that the military buildup is
> not going to be stopped by ... those who oppose
> military increases now. They're just a small,
> small percentage of the population. While a

lot of peace groups will talk about getting
more rank-and-file blue collar worker people
involved ... by doing our work, we're making
their job easier because people begin to see
the links. I always describe our work to
people as enlarging the whole arena of
political actors. We're getting people who ...
have never defined themselves as being
politically inclined, whatever, ... so we're
enlarging the progressive end of the political
spectrum.

The limits on issues that Boston ACORN can address stem from
several factors. First, there is the above-mentioned problem of
concreteness:

On the issues where there is the least amount
of consensus, they're also the issues that are
the hardest to grasp campaign-wise in some
ways; they're not concrete, day-to-day things
that affect our members' lives. Although you
might argue that abortion certainly affects our
members' lives. But questions about military
aid in Central America and defense spending
[are] less a part of peoples' day-to-day
living. We ... avoid getting heavily involved
in those issues for that reason as much as
because there's a lack of consensus on them.

The organizer quoted above also expressed the ideal of
reconciling broad issues with the daily concerns of members under
specific circumstances:

I also ... think that on the membership side
that there's a difference between peoples'
intellectual responses to things like that and
peoples' responses after some amount of
discussion or context put to the questions.
Our board voted to endorse the Central American
Referendum that was on the ballot in Boston
last fall after a fair amount of discussion on
it. Because it was tied to domestic spending
and ... social programs, and when people make
those connections there tends to be more of a
consensus on where that issue should go than
when it's talked about in a vacuum.

The second limit cited by the organizers is the problem of natural divisions among their constituents: race, gender, and ethnicity. One of the organizers voiced an acute awareness of the limits imposed by the differences within ACORN's class-based constituency:

> I think it's important that left-wing organizations address the special needs of minorities, Blacks, Hispanics. ACORN's existence promotes those rights, but we don't really raise those issues ..., affirmative action, pro choice, ... or anything like that. Our existence helps those organizations that do, but we don't, mainly because it would split the organization ... We were working on a police protection campaign and right in the middle of it this kid was killed by a cop ... Of course, all the Whites said, "Oh yeah, a Puerto Rican, he stole a car, so they should have shot him." A lot of Puerto Ricans, and even some Blacks, were charging police brutality. Most of our leadership felt that way too, though we didn't raise that banner, although we did work with the Puerto Rican group that was involved with the campaign. At one point, we had a number of our White members walk out of a hearing where the issue of police brutality was raised. That wasn't even raised by ACORN, this was raised by some other organization. You could see what would happen if those issues were raised. One of the reasons that ACORN has really failed to see that it's not just a class issue, there are issues of race that generate excitement among the minorities, and you have to address those issues, too.

The other limit that the organizers discussed is created by the necessities of ACORN's organizing style. Since the constituency responds to short-term, concrete issues and campaigns, the organizing style itself places limits on the kinds of issues the organization works on:

> [Many issues] just don't fit into the base. When I go out on the doors with people and ask what they'd like to see better, ... I never hear anybody say, "Stop killer cops." I've

never heard anybody say that. But what we ask
doesn't lead to statements like that. We ask
what they want to see improved on their block,
around their neighborhood.

Of course we're ignoring things we should look
at. I don't know what we've ever done about
healthcare in a major way. We've been able to
pack hearings so hospitals remain open in
low-income areas, things like that. But so
much of what ACORN does is so short-term. We
don't have the time, or the staff, or the
leisure to really approach basic problems ...

Nevertheless, within the issue agenda the organization
pursues, the organizers claim there is significant flexibility on
which ones should be dealt with at any given time:

In part, it depends on what prompted the change
[in the agenda]. In one of our local groups
recently, we kind of put on hold a campaign on
asbestos in the schools. To a degree, because
the organizer was really frustrated about the
campaign. But we also put it on hold because
there was a twenty-story, 168-unit elderly
high-rise run by the Boston Housing Authority
that had two elevators that were always broken
down. We actually cancelled a meeting on the
asbestos issue. We called people back and said
... we've cancelled this meeting, this action
is going on the day after tomorrow, we need
your help in it ... I don't think anybody got
terribly upset. One thing you have to remember
is that most of the issues that our members are
concerned about have been hitting them in the
face for a long, long time. If they don't see
progress over some long term, then it does
become a problem.

Most of the primary and secondary leadership
see the main goals of the organization, not so
much the neighborhood issues. So, if we drop
everything and work on the Dallas trip [to the
ACORN 1984 National Convention], the members
will get behind the idea that we have to spend
more time on Dallas and less time on vacant
lots.

This flexibility, they claim, stems from the long-standing nature of unresolved grievances in their lives, organizational commitment, and a broader, more abstract, view of issues.

These statements center on a recurring theme: the organizers' desire to generate left-wing progressive political issues is limited by the narrower, more concrete political vision of their constituents. The organizers claim that these limits can be expanded by creative organizing and by the members' commitment to the organization. In fact, the expansion of their constituents' limits seems to be one of the major goals of ACORN organizers.

Views on Tactics

Several of the questions in the interview asked the ACORN organizers to discuss the kinds of tactics they thought were the most desirable and effective. Because ACORN literature emphasizes that it is a "direct action" organization I asked why confrontational tactics are important, what effect they have on members, what tactics members prefer, and if organizers have philosophical commitments to confrontational tactics. Once again, the critical question becomes: What technique is the most effective for promoting low- and moderate-income membership and participation in a political organization? Clearly, the tactics the organization adopts to achieve its goals comprise a major portion of the constituents' experience as members -- and therefore assume a critical role in the organization's success.

The organizers expressed a preference for confrontational tactics in their organizing for a variety of reasons: their educational effects on the members, the excitement they generate, their salutary effects on the organization, and their impact on everyone involved. However, the organizers noted that they must choose tactics strategically. That is, they must apply the tactic that will be most effective at the particular moment, for their current campaign. Moreover, the organizers noted that there are costs for confrontational tactics, even when applied appropriately.

ACORN campaigns follow a natural progression that begins with requests for action on an issue. For example, ACORN might ask that a city agency clear vacant lots in an ACORN neighborhood. If the members are not satisfied with the response they receive, they become more direct and forceful:

You just have to think organizationally, what's

68

gonna be best for us. If bargaining or
building a coalition is going to advance your
cause, fine, but if that fails, then you have
to confront people. That's one of the reasons
that ACORN is here -- to confront people with
received opinions, to confront their ... very
comfortability ...

While the organizers prefer the more direct tactics, they
recognize that the members do not want to be confrontational
until the target has had an opportunity to respond to their
non-confrontational requests first:

People say, "Well, let's not go out to his
house yet. Let's do this or that first." It's
always harder to drive people toward
militance. It would be far easier for me to
stomach ... a tactic that I didn't think would
be effective, because that's a one-shot deal.
If you take a particular type of action and it
doesn't work, on the whole that can be a very
positive experience for the group. It can show
them that in fact you do need to be militant.
In fact, six hundred names on a petition hasn't
moved this asshole. We've gotta do something
else. I know a lot of times we do an action we
know isn't going to be effective but it will
build peoples' commitment and involvement ...

Despite the organizers' preference for confrontational
tactics, one cited a case in his experience in which
non-confrontational tactics were preferable:

You build the organization more in the sense by
confrontational tactics, though, at the same
time, cooperative tactics can be good, I mean
it depends on what you're trying to achieve.
Cooperative tactics ... can be very effective.
I've been dealing with vacant lots [since
starting with ACORN] and we're trying to get
some funding from the federal government or the
city for a landscaping project. And that's
definitely cooperative tactics. It's gonna be
the members doing most of the work, planting
the seeds and all that. Rather than getting
the city to do it. In that sense, we're
getting money from the federal structure of the

> group to get money from the city ... so the
> group is useful for that. Some people take
> leadership in that project and are definitely
> developing their leadership there ...

Clearly, organizers apply tactics as they fit strategies, but
confrontational tactics are seen as the most desirable. The
organizers cited four basic reasons why confrontational tactics
are the most effective for the long term: educational effects,
excitement, organization-building, and impact. Obviously, if
ACORN organizers are trying to broaden their constituents' view
of politics, the educational effects of a tactic would be an
important consideration:

> It's ... the best way to educate the members.
> When there's a lot of conflict ... that's when
> people change their ideas, that's when new
> leaders come forward, people that aren't really
> into the organization. You can't be
> super-militant all the time, but you have to be
> able to pull off militant actions, and the most
> militant actions possible. That's the only way
> to get anywhere.

Two organizers noted that confrontational tactics are
particularly useful for educating members about the organizers'
perceptions of the nature of authorities:

> They're more polarizing. If you get somebody
> at a neighborhood ACORN meeting and you're
> giving him or her a real hard time, either
> they're going to cave in or they're going to
> become more defensive and sort of lash out, and
> that's really important because it shows our
> members [that] in the heat of confrontation
> people say things they really don't intend to
> say and it shows our members their true colors
> sometimes. They'll make some terrible slur
> about poor people or something ... and the
> members will learn that when push comes to
> shove, everybody else is going to stand up for
> his own self-interest and therefore you can't
> believe him when he says, "Gee, I'd really like
> to help you guys ..." So that's a tremendous
> benefit.

We went to the BRA [Boston Redevelopment

70

Authority] and the BRA director was <u>furious</u> and
it was good to see him get that angry. Because
his notions of order had been drastically
rearranged. And it was good for us because he
was arrogant, rude, and condescending, and that
helps us all the time.

Thus, by stimulating conflict and forcing a situation in which
officers feel threatened and become less diplomatic, organizers
feel that members will have an opportunity to see what
powerholders truly think about ACORN members and their
grievances.

The organizers also claim that the excitement of
confrontational tactics generated also makes them more
desirable. They described the experience in terms of the feeling
of power that it creates for both members and organizers.

I'm sure people remember confrontational longer
... than ... bargaining or negotiating. I
think confrontation is a lot more fun. That's
one of the reasons that I like this job, for
the fun, sometimes.

Confrontational tactics also help keep the
staff going. You can literally see targets
sweat, sometimes. And you feel pressure you
<u>know</u> they never, ever feel.

The one street-blocking that I did, the people
... thought it was fun. One man, who I just
assumed wouldn't come, came, and [while]
everyone else was sort of milling around he was
the one who got the ball rolling saying, "Well,
I can give them some garbage," and then he
began throwing things out on the street. He
had such a good time doing that! It felt like
you were nine years old. Everyone had fun.
The house visits were fun ... they're a little
afraid to do those, but once things got moving
and once a couple of people took charge, people
after the fact ... tend to think they were more
fun than when they were doing it.

One organizer cited what he believes are organizational
benefits from confrontational tactics:

Confrontational tactics also help determine
who's really a good leader. A lot of people
sit on the front porch and rant and rave about
the assholes down at City Hall and when they
get down there they're quiet and meek as a
mouse. Again, when you have a 58-year-old
woman standing two feet from the mayor shaking
her finger at him and all this stuff and two
days later the vacant lots get cut, everybody
in the room knows that it wasn't coincidence.
So that's yet another benefit.

In other words, besides providing clear and tangible benefits for
time and energy involved in ACORN activism, direct action helps
to separate the sheep from the goats, helping to determine
individual members' degree of commitment.

The organizers' discussions of the impact of confrontational
tactics on members and targets identified two valuable results:
(1) targets are moved, and (2) members feel satisfaction. The
effectiveness of confrontational tactics was perceived as
critical:

The ones that are the most militant are the
best ... You've always got the ... sort of ...
"bad guys," the people [targets] that are
extreme, but then you've got people who are
sort of trying to do something. As far as
tactics for the "bad guys," militant tactics
are the best because that's the only way you're
ever gonna get them to listen to you, that's
the only way you'll get them to do something.

The more militant the better. It's just so
hard to move people toward those things in a
lot of ways. And yet, when we do, we almost
inevitably win. If we hadn't squatted, we
would be nowhere on the homesteading.

While effectiveness and satisfaction are not entirely distinct
categories -- there is a lot of satisfaction in winning --
organizers described significant satisfaction apart from or in
addition to success:

I think the more militant, the more popular.
People really feel like ... they're much more
satisfied with really giving hell to some

72

official than being nice to them and not
getting anything out of it. We went down to
the HUD office and really got into a shouting
match with HUD, the head of the Northeast
Region ..., calling him a liar and a bastard,
people were swearing at each other and
everything, and maybe we went a little too far,
but people came out feeling much better about
that than if they had gone down and been really
nice to him and still not accomplished
anything.

The   organizers' evaluations of confrontational tactics are
not all   positive.   Given peoples' preference for dignity and
decorum,   confrontational tactics have cost ACORN members at
times:

A small "down" is that once in a while we lost
some of our more mild-mannered members who feel
we've been too tough on a target, particularly
if they come in on the fourth action of a
campaign and this is their first action. They
tend to think, "Gosh, why are people being so
rowdy?" And they ... weren't paying attention
during the prep session or they didn't really
believe earlier when they said he wouldn't
return our phone calls ... and that's why we're
taking this step.

People tend to just eliminate themselves
without a lot of conflict. Going to someone's
house or doing a street-blocking, you always
lose people. We did a street-blocking and a
woman who was very active and attended a lot of
meetings just won't have anything to do with us
anymore. She hasn't come out and said it, but
she hasn't been to a single meeting since. And
she's very cool and noncommittal on the phone
now ... And so you just can't please everyone
and change things. You have to offend
somebody.

Organizers believe this same preference for dignified behavior
operates when outsiders observe ACORN's confrontational behavior:

And we're getting into situations where anybody
got arrested or anything like that. That would

73

> be a disadvantage. Legal fees ... and
> depending on how the press made it look, ...
> you know, "troublemakers" ... but even if you
> get arrested, it can make them look bad.

> And there's the larger picture in which the
> public perception of ACORN is we're a bunch of
> crazies, we do what the general public regards
> as some outlandish things. But that's not a
> particularly compelling argument against doing
> militant tactics ... We've got to be true to
> our membership rather than some amorphous group
> of people that haven't done anything but read a
> newspaper.

Finally, the organizers noted that, since confrontational
tactics require greater commitment, better preparation, and
widespread agreement on the goal and the tactics, their use makes
cooperative ventures with other organizations much more
difficult:

> ACORN tends to "Lone Ranger" it a lot. And, I
> think, for really good reasons. What ACORN
> does best is direct action, and a lot of groups
> simply don't like to do that. And if you get
> involved with coalitions and if you need a
> consensus for what you're going to do, other
> groups are pointless. And if you get wrapped
> up in coalitions, you dilute whatever strength
> you have.

Thus, despite the drawbacks the organizers cited, they
prefer confrontational tactics for the benefits they provide the
members, the organizers, and the organization. While they do not
and cannot use confrontation indiscriminately, its effectiveness,
its ability to shake things up, and its educational value make it
a desirable choice of tactics.

The Decision Making Process

The organizers recognize the importance of the decision
making process to the quality of their work. They convey a
professional concern for the manner in which important decisions
are made, first, because they are sensitive to past criticisms
that they control the organization and, second, because they feel
that the place to start educating low- and moderate-income people
in political activism is within their own organization.

Consequently, responses to the questions regarding the decision
making process generally stressed the complexity of the process
and the need to strive for the ideal of member control.

Responses of organizers to the question, "Who makes the
decisions in Boston ACORN?" were quite consistent:

> Different kinds of staff and different kinds of
> membership -- the head organizer, the
> rank-and-file organizer, the leadership of the
> members, and the rank-and-file of the members.
> In terms of who makes the decisions, you can't
> pinpoint one of those four elements as making a
> decision. It's hard to say, because I don't
> want to say the members make all the decisions
> because it simply is not true.

> It's sort of like ... the decisions are made by
> the leaders, and the leaders are the leaders in
> the organization and also the staff help make
> decisions, but always in consultation with the
> leadership of the group. And those decisions
> are always made in the context of what the
> feeling in the broad membership is, or
> perceived to be.

> I think the staff has more power than it
> should. Probably because it's more expedient
> to think of something yourself and raise it
> with the membership in such a way that they'll
> think it's a good idea. Or even if you have a
> couple of choices, they're the choices the
> staff picks, sometimes.

> Formally, our executive board does, which meets
> once a month, but in reality, organizers have a
> <u>tremendous</u> amount of influence. Some things
> that we get involved with arise strictly out of
> membership, things the best organizers would
> never have even thought of.

> ... [T]he structure of the organization is such
> where even if staff is pushing for certain
> decisions nothing's going to get carried out
> that the members aren't into. There's no
> question the final say comes out of the board
> and the leadership and that the members

perceive the staff as working for them, for the organization.

Organizers clearly have a lot of power within the organization, but there are important checks on their power.

One of the most important checks is the desire expressed by the organizers to develop the members' skills and commitment by making sure _they_ are the ones making important decisions. The recurring theme throughout the interviews is that the most effective organizers are the ones who delegate as much as possible and confer with the members as much as possible, thereby diluting their control over the decision making process. Delegating power and responsibility is a major topic and ideal expressed by the organizers:

> [T]he times that I've grown most as an organizer and developed is when I've tried to juggle two or three local group campaigns at one time. By taking on that additional load, it's forced me to prod, push, pull, whatever, our members into doing more. And that's what it's all about, I think. If we take fewer [issues] we take more of the load as organizers and therefore we don't empower people as much as we should. There's always a temptation to do more of the job ourselves than we really need to be doing.

> Allowing them to take part of the organization, allowing them to take part of the agenda, allowing them to speak at a public hearing, chair a meeting, just in any of the million different ways of things you need to do to get an organization going. By letting the members participate as fully as possible, by delegating a lot of the stuff the organizer has to do to all the members. That really builds peoples' sense of ownership of the organization.

> It's very interesting to me ... the degree to which we push membership ownership of the organization. And getting leaders involved in a real serious way. Something we could certainly do more of, and every time we do more of it, it's wonderful for both the leaders and the members. I think that _may_ be one of our

76

shortcomings. We do need to make a concerted effort, just constantly, to get members to be doing things that they certainly are capable of doing and that we certainly don't <u>need</u> to be doing. I wouldn't recommend that everybody be stuck in an office for six months by themselves, but the benefits of that were just tremendous. It made me feel somewhat foolish for not having part of the members do more.

The process of conferring with members and leaders is critical to the proper practice of professional organizing, according to the organizers interviewed:

Obviously, the organizer is playing some kind of leadership role. People, for good reason, are suspicious of outsiders in the community. One time, me and the staff director ... thought it was a good idea to go ahead and move a campaign about something ... and said, "Let's do it, we gotta do <u>something</u>. There's all these people out there that want something to happen." And we didn't really involve the leader in the discussion. And we went ahead and did it and she got all upset about it and how we bypassed her, even though it was a good thing and she came, she thought it was a bad way to do it.

I think conflict comes out of a lack of communication, when organizers stop listening to the members ... and make assumptions. It's a fine line the organizers are walking sometimes, and that part of what happens ... is that organizers ... expect ... members to pull the reins. It shouldn't work like that. The organizers, <u>themselves</u>, should be from the get-go just asking the questions and making sure that they're structuring things so it is the members making the decisions. Sometimes it happens almost out of convenience ... an organizer knows this is what the group needs or we want to build the group in this way, so it'll be quicker if I just make things happen.

Thus, although the potential for organizer control of decision making exists, the organizers are sensitive to criticism and express professional ethics that counter that tendency to some extent.

The organizers agree that the process requires member involvement for decisions to be effective.

> The organizers will talk to the members and leaders about [a campaign]. The average organizer talks to ten or twelve times more people about neighborhood issues than even our best leader does. So if there is something that's happening, ... [an organizer] will find out about it sometimes before the neighborhood leaders will.

> In one of the groups I have, they have this playground that's filled with winos, it's just across the street from a liquor store. I didn't all of a sudden decide to work on that like no one else had thought to do it before. People for years have been trying to do something about that. And if you say that to someone and the group will say, "Yeah, that's a good idea." Then you mention it to everyone else, you have a campaign going. I wouldn't say that I made a decision to do that. If people had said it's a bad idea, we just wouldn't have done it ... but certainly there's power in the fact that you're a catalyst, that you're certainly the one that's bringing people together. That's powerful. But on the other hand, people won't be brought together for a reason they don't think is good. So you're always held in check.

> [Y]ou have a planning meeting before we have a big meeting or an action or anything like that, and for the planning meeting, in theory, the organizer who's pulling it together is supposed to consult with all the different leaders, five or six leaders, and find out what the key issues are, work on getting the agenda together, finding out what people think we should do ... and at the planning meeting pretty much make a decision on what we're gonna do, or else, or at least the rough guidelines of what we're gonna do. Then we have a big

neighborhood meeting where people from the whole community meet to ratify the ideas of the planning meeting. It's a process between the leaders ... and the mass of the membership. The final outcome is dependent on how it is accepted or how people react to it.

In terms of the issues to work on, I believe it's really the membership that decides the issues to work on. The way that can happen is that some people can talk about some issue and others get more excited about those issues at meetings. The organizers sort of transmit those issues to other members and see what they think. In that sense we're sure to get a lot of people involved in the issues that we work on.

Thus, for the organizers to promote a decision making process which generates excitement and enthusiasm for the organization, they must consult with the members and leaders in a variety of ways: on the doors, while planning meetings, and in the meetings. While all of the organizers recognized that they and other organizers in Boston ACORN possessed and exercised power, they also recognized that ideally they should do so as sparingly as possible, for both ethical and practical reasons.

Summary

The organizers interviewed considered themselves professionals in a field that requires both expertise and responsiveness to their constituents. Their responses indicated that their motives combined a progressive political agenda with the opportunity to empower low- and moderate-income people. The organization attempts to reconcile the contradictions of these goals in the way it provides incentives to the members, pursues its goals, and makes its important decisions.

By the organizers' admission, the process is imperfect. Yet the organizers claim to hold professional standards of practice and ethics. They attempt to promote the issues they, as left-wing political activists, believe in, yet preserve the democratic control of the organization for the membership. The interviews with the members and insights by the researcher and writers on the topic of community organizing will examine their claim in chapters to come.

C H A P T E R   V

THE MEMBERS

This chapter will discuss the results of interviews with
ACORN members and compare them with the goals of the ACORN
organizing strategy. The interviews explored: member
characteristics, their views on why they and others join and
participate in ACORN, their perceptions of the group's decision
making process, their views on American politics and political
issues, their sense of how ACORN's purposes activate members to
contribute, and their perceptions of ACORN's tactics.

The members' responses enable us to evaluate the impact of
ACORN organizing on the constituency. They also provide insights
into the questions raised by the literature and the problems
faced by the political organizers.*

The Characteristics of the Interviewees

The nineteen members interviewed are but a small part of the
2,500 total Boston ACORN members. They do, however, represent a
fairly large portion of the more active members and officers of
the organization. Among the people interviewed were ten
officeholders, the Massachusetts representative to the ACORN
National Board, and eight members who have attended national
ACORN conventions. The demographic characteristics of the
interviewees are quite different from the average political
activist, however. Eighteen of the members are black, one is
white. Seventeen are women. The age and education levels of the
members are presented in Table 5-1. Six of the interviewees are
retired, two are on welfare or disability, and eleven are
employed full-time. Only four of them have spouses and nearly
all have children. Thus, the group is predominantly black,
female, older, high school educated, employed or retired, and

---

*The quotes are an attempt to reproduce the language used by
the interviewee as closely as possible. The text of the
interview responses will include grammatical errors and
underlining to express emphasis where the interviewee was clearly
intending to emphasize a word or phrase.

TABLE 5-1

AGE AND EDUCATION OF INTERVIEWEES

Age	Number	Education Level	Number
18-25	1	Grade school	1
26-31	2	Some high school	3
32-39	4	High school diploma	7
40-49	3	Some college	3
50-59	2	College degree	3
Over 61	7	Graduate or professional training	2

single. In marked contrast, the Boston ACORN organizers are all white, single, childless, and college-educated. Moreover, they are considerably younger, between twenty-one and thirty-two, and only one was a woman. Hence, the demographic data is important not only in terms of how similar individuals tend to behave politically, but also in terms of the differences between members and organizers.

The participation rates of most of the interviewees are quite high, though there was some mix of relative newcomers or people who have remained somewhat on the fringes of the organization. The activities members reported break down into four categories, from those most frequently engaged in to those that are not often engaged in. Table 5-2 gives the data on participation rates in these activities. The interviewees participated in an average of 9.47 activities; the range was from one to all eighteen activities. Nine of the interviewees are very active, six active, and four not active. Nine might be called "charter members" of Boston ACORN, joining during the first round of organizing in 1980. Thus, the group interviewed comes primarily from the most active, most knowledgeable and most committed segment of the organization, and the responses generally reflect the experiences and insights of long-term members who have participated frequently and in a wide variety of activities.

The Membership Decision

Responses to the question, "Why did you join ACORN?", fell into four major categories: service to community, serving others, specific issues, and self-development. Few interviewees

TABLE 5-2

ACTIVITIES IN WHICH INTERVIEWEES ENGAGED

Frequency	Activity	No. Who Engaged
Most frequent	Raised funds	17
	Phoned	17
	Marched in action	16
Very frequent	Distributed flyers	14
	Recruited members	13
	Campaigned in election	12
	Served on APAC	12
Less frequent	Held office	10
	Chaired meeting	10
	Recruited in public	9
	Attended national convention	8
	Doorknocked	8
Least frequent	Led action	7
	Hosted meeting in home	7
	Attended national action	7
	Attended public hearing	6
	Signed support letter	6

restricted their answer to one reason, and some of those cited other reasons in response to other questions in the interview. Hence, few of the ACORN members made the membership decision for only one reason. Rather, they were attracted to the organization for a variety of things. Interestingly, few of the interviewees joined for clearly self-interested reasons, referring instead to broader concerns.

The respondents that cited community or neighborhood improvement, for example, discussed issues such as beautification, safety, and crime. Beautification included cleaning up weeds and trash in vacant lots, removing abandoned cars, and developing park areas. Safety issues involved traffic controls at dangerous intersections, WALK signals for pedestrians, and abandoned buildings that threaten children's safety and present fire hazards. They addressed crime issues by their desire to rid the area of buildings that are used as drug hangouts, or that offer opportunities for rapists to hide and commit crimes. They were also concerned with street corners or parking lots in which people regularly gather to drink, and dark streets in need of lighting.

The typical ACORN neighborhood has an abundance of potential issues due to poor city services in lower-income, and especially black, areas. The ACORN technique of doorknocking virtually always uncovers issues that organizers can use to recruit members. Eleven of the interviewees cited reasons of community improvement for originally joining ACORN.

Two members stated that they joined ACORN in order to help others. They welcomed the opportunity to get involved in a program to do "something to help the poor." Several described ACORN as a service organization like the Eastern Star (and were, in fact, members of that organization also). They joined to help those less fortunate than themselves to obtain housing, health care, public safety and other necessities. For example, several were involved in a campaign to improve a nearby elderly high-rise.

Several members said that they were originally interested in ACORN because it gave them an opportunity to get involved in an interesting organization and engage in new and educational activities. They felt that it would improve the quality of their lives via community involvement, expanded horizons and chances to meet interesting people. They expressed a need to find an outlet for excess energy or extra time in their lives, a need that arose when they experienced changes in their lives such as a move into a new neighborhood or their children leaving home. One woman said she joined ACORN for two reasons:

> Number one, to get out of the house; number two, it's interesting. It's very interesting. You learn about other things, other people, how they are doing, how they felt.

Another responded similarly:

> I really joined because of my daughter. She was growing up. She was my last daughter ... I know pretty soon she was going to be leaving home and I said, "I've got to do something for myself that's interesting to me instead of staying home and being bored all the time."

Perhaps this motivation explains why so many of the members are

retired or older people, looking for stimulation once
childraising and work no longer occupy their minds and energies.

Finally, at least five respondents mentioned specific issues
that do not fall into the above categories. Most of these were
interested in housing, a major campaign in Boston ACORN. Several
wanted to obtain housing for themselves. One woman stated: "I
got tired of renting and it got so high. And I want a house of
my own." A woman who was already in a HUD program stated: "I
was having a problem with housing. I went to ACORN. Someone had
given me the information that ACORN was helping the tenants get
results." For one interviewee, health care was the attraction to
ACORN:

> I got involved because of the health care issue
> ... They had started to let over half the staff
> go [at the local community health program where
> she brings her children] and say to us that
> they would still give the same health care. We
> know that wasn't possible.

Thus, in addition to place-related and self-improvement issues,
ACORN has appealed to people with individual economic problems,
particularly housing.

ACORN therefore appears to fill a variety of needs. Much of
the same response came when members were asked about attempts to
recruit new members, though neighborhood issues were more
frequently noted here. Thirteen respondents emphasized the
importance of stressing the benefits ACORN brings to the
community or neighborhood. One woman said:

> I tell them it actually is an organization that
> is here to help with anything that you feel as
> though you can't stand in the neighborhood.
> You can call the office at any time and put in
> your complaint. And if it's something we can
> handle, it'll come up at the meeting and we can
> handle it.

Another responded: "They need to belong to something that is
concerned with the neighborhood and community. They do come into
the neighborhoods." Four members emphasized the opportunities to
satisfy personal needs. At the same time, they made it clear
that this could only be done by actively participating in the
pursuit of needed services or goods:

I explain to them that it is a self-help
program. A lot of people expect that you pay
"X" amount of money per year and you want
something done, you come to ACORN and ACORN
does it for you. But it's people -- ACORN is
people. Getting together and getting things
done.

I tell them that when you come in you don't
come in expecting the board to do your work
that you want done. Because you are ACORN. As
though when you come in there, you have to be
the one coming out, and if there's something
coming up, you have to get it done because you
are ACORN. There's a lot of misunderstanding
among people -- "I want ACORN to do this, I
want ACORN to do that" -- ACORN cannot do
that. You are ACORN. You come, and ACORN
joins along with you. You have to work with
us, you can't say, "This didn't get done, that
didn't get done." In other words, you have to
work with it, in it, and I do that. And I tell
them that.

Finally, the respondents noted the effectiveness of recruiting
new members by emphasizing the opportunities to help others:

It's helpful to others, a chance to help others
... and serve themselves. To get knowledge, to
know how to handle certain things in their
life.

Thus, the respondents feel that the incentives that were
effective in recruiting them into ACORN are also the ones most
likely to persuade new people to make that same membership
decision, confirming that their experiences in ACORN have met
their original expectations.

Why People Stay

Members find satisfaction in their ACORN experiences that
run the gamut from solidary incentives to purposive incentives.
In the course of the interviews, virtually every kind of
incentive available to a political organization was articulated
in some fashion by the interviewees. They expressed satisfaction
in: working with other members, gaining status by their
association with ACORN, learning about politics and the world,

86

improving their neighborhood, helping others, making their lives easier, contributing to a worthy cause, fighting against a common foe, and so on.

Solidary incentives were clearly expressed by several of the members. One woman referred to ACORN as "a friendly organization where everybody is friendly and everybody tries to help one another. [They] try to be cautious of everybody going home in the evening after the meetings all by themselves." One woman went as far as describing ACORN as "a big family. It's a very friendly bunch of people and they're concerned about what's going on in their areas. No matter how small one might think it is, it's of importance."

An individual whose social and ethnic background differed greatly from the main body of the ACORN membership stated:

> A lot of it is social -- I met a lot of nice people, the organizers, the members. I've met people whom I never would have met before. The fact is, I never went to Roxbury, and in the last three years, I've been to situations where I've been the only white man present. And there's never been any unpleasantness.

One member also reported solidary incentives in the form of status:

> I've gained a lot of ground with ACORN. I've traveled places that I probably would have never gotten to travel. I've had a lot of good experience with them. I even got a chance to be on the platform with a presidential candidate. And I watched 80-, 90,000 wishful people wishing they could be there. And I got there through ACORN and I'm telling you it was electrifying, it really was. I was in like another world. I got to embrace Senator Kennedy who you'll probably never see unless you talk to an aide and he'll say what he <u>said</u> but you're never gonna get near these people, but I was right there, feeling just as important as they were. All through ACORN.

Material incentives clearly play a role in keeping members involved in the organization. A woman, whose primary motive for joining was to obtain housing, was asked why she stays involved

87

though she has succeeded in her original intentions: "We gotta stay on HUD to be sure they do all the repairs. Hot water, holes in the hallways, no security, no bells, leaks ..." Another respondent expressed satisfaction at the material successes within the neighborhood:

> It gets a little more interesting every time we accomplish something. And one thing that came to light yesterday ... was the fact that we had worked, and we worked very hard up here with blocking the street up here, because we want a streetlight up here. And to my surprise, this weekend, we do have a traffic cop there. We have accomplished the fact that the police have been out.

Hence, material incentives provide satisfaction both at the individual level and the collective level.

Purposive incentives were also among the responses of several of the members. The satisfaction of working toward a goal with the organization was revealed in statements such as:

> I get a great deal of satisfaction knowing that I'm involved with this particular thing, and that some good can come out of it and it's not just for me, it's for everybody. I do like doing things in conjunction with other people, dealing with other people's concerns, not only mine. What's good for me is good for my neighbor.

Another member expressed the sentiment that:

> ACORN is the kind of organization that ... we fight for what we really want. At first I thought it was a place ... like a church that just began, it is just a place where people go to talk over their problems. It's not that. People don't go there to discuss their problems, they go there to try to help other people that have problems like police problems, like the police should solve but they don't.

Hence, it is clear that, for some of the members, the organization provides an opportunity to work on issues for the general good -- to influence public policy. Thus ACORN organizing does not limit itself to one or several of the incentives available to such an organization. Rather, it provides all of those incentives in an effort to maintain members' desire to stay and participate in the organization. ACORN does not depend on any one form of incentive. In fact, for any type of incentive, there was a respondent who articulated the importance of each incentive for ACORN's ability to attract and maintain its members.

Democracy in the Decision Making Process

Most of the recent literature on grassroots organizing stresses the importance of a participatory and democratic decision making process. Respondents offered several views on the level of membership control of ACORN's decision making process. The dominant response, however, was that ACORN is a democratic organization with an open agenda, debate on important issues, and a fair voting process. Twelve of the respondents said that the members make the important decisions in ACORN; two said it is a cooperative effort between members and organizers; one said that organizers make the decisions; four said they did not know. Naturally, the less active respondents expressed no opinion, but the other respondents were equally divided among the active and less active members.

The interviewees who claimed that decisions are made democratically were enthusiastic in their support for the process:

> The members. All the members. They have a chance to voice their opinion.

> Everybody has their say. And then they decide. We all sit around there, and we say, "you think we wanna do so-and-so-and-so-and-so?" And then she go around and ask, "What are you gonna think about this? Do you think we should do so-and-so-and-so-and-so, or shouldn't we do so-and-so-and-so-and-so?" That's the way they do. It's very democratic, you can say whatever you wanna say. At the meetings. I don't know what goes on further up, but they must do it the very same way. We decide, the members themselves ... what we gonna do, and how we gonna do it.

> You set up a meeting on a particular issue and

> we have the members come in, especially the
> board members ... and they'll talk about the
> issue that is at hand and they'll come out with
> what we would like to see obtained from this
> meeting. This how the goals are set ...

Some members were more critical and either qualified their
belief in member control or felt that organizers had more control
over decision making than they should. One suggested that
organizers were responsible for setting the agenda:

> The organizers put it on the table and ask us
> whether or not we will support or not support a
> group. We discuss it, if there are any
> questions, if we do or we don't agree with it,
> like when they mentioned rent control, whether
> or not we'd support it, I had a problem with
> it, supporting rent control. Everybody looked
> at me like "this" and I said there's some new
> rules so I don't mind once they explained them
> to me.

Several went further and suggested that organizers dominate the
organization and should give the members more control of
important decisions:

> The organizers will maintain their control in
> the organization. It's not their place. To
> me, it is not their place. It's up to the
> members to get things going. And I hate to see
> them always say, "Oh, let's organize." What
> about us, can't we free the organizers up?

> My observation has been it is frequently the
> organizers [who make the decisions] ... One of
> my objections has been that they frequently sit
> down and talk with themselves and then try to
> convince the membership. I think, sometimes,
> that as well-meaning as the organizers are,
> they should listen to what the membership has
> to say. It's easy to convince someone who's
> participating for the first time rather than
> sit down and talk and get his input and let him
> make up his mind. It may not get done as well
> or as quickly, if you have to get some eighth
> grade dropout to do a particular task, but,
> ultimately, that should be the way a democratic

organization works -- the membership not only
pay their dues, but they participate in the
decision making and on-going tasks.

Hence, given the opportunity to criticize the decision making
process or praise it, nearly all the members praised it.

Members were also asked how they felt when decisions on
three areas of ACORN activity are made counter to their wishes:
issues, support for candidates in elections, and tactics.   The
intent behind splitting these responses was to give ample
opportunity for interviewees to express their ideas and to jog
their memories for specific events. The responses fell into four
basic categories: (1) dissent and abstention from the activity;
(2) expression of disagreement;   (3) disagreement and then
consenting to majority wishes; and (4) keeping quiet about any
disagreement.

The most common response was for members to abstain from
participating in decisions with which they disagreed:

> That's happened once or twice. For example,
> the post card registration -- I just don't
> believe in that. I just don't assist in
> organizing for that issue. And I don't think
> they expect anyone to support an issue where
> they have some objection or philosophical
> objection.

> Well, I still have to work to maintain unity.
> If I didn't agree on it, the majority wins. As
> I said, we take a vote on it. And if twelve
> members are there, and I'm three, nine want it,
> three don't, I'm one of the three, then, you
> know, I have to go along with the board. I'll
> support it. That doesn't mean I'll work on it,
> but I'll support it.

> More than likely I won't support them. It goes
> back to the type of person I am. I would say,
> "No, you can forget me this time. I'll catch
> you when you get something else. I don't feel
> like you doing the right thing."

> That has happened. And I have managed to kind
> of work around that. As they were working with
> different candidates. So I get to work with a

91

candidate that I <u>liked</u>. That has happened.

Thus, these members express their views and act on them by absenting themselves from the organization's activities, a form of democratic choice.

The second response, disagreement, contains an element of obligation on the dissenter's part. The following statements express a readiness to dissent openly and clearly as a part of the decision making process:

> I'd tell 'em. That's as far as I'd go with that. Do you mean would I pull out? If it bothered me enough I'd just disagree with them, that's all.

> I would tell them. The majority wins when you start, you know. If they decided and I didn't agree with it, then I'd let them know I didn't agree with it, that's all. I wouldn't say that I'd win. But just like everything else, I'm entitled to my opinion. If I didn't like what they was doing, then I wouldn't agree with them. [What if you lost?] I'd just drop it. If the vote went against me and the majority won, I'd still support it.

> Everything's supposed to have a leader, yes, but you're not supposed to be a blind follower. If you disagree, disagree. It's a democracy; you're entitled to your own opinion.

Interestingly, these interviewees expressed the willingness to go along with the decision once the process had been followed. This sentiment was most clearly expressed in the following statement:

> If I'm outvoted, then I go along with the organization. Because I realize that no matter how strong <u>I</u> feel like, it doesn't make it the best way to do it. So I go with the majority.

Thus, the members seem generally willing to exercise their rights to dissent within ACORN. Failing that, they recognize the opportunity to dissent by abstaining from whatever activity they wish to.

Despite the eagerness many expressed to dissent when they

were not agreeing with the ideas that were being considered, one member took a rather different view of the role of the dissenter:

> I guess I would just have to keep quiet. There's too many members for me to be the one to persuade anybody. A decision would be made by the three communities [Roxbury, Dorchester, and Mattapan].

The existence of conflict reflects on the degree of democracy in an organization. I asked if there was any persistent conflict between participants in ACORN. Few interviewees felt there is any serious conflict; only five could identify any significant conflict in Boston ACORN. Of these, none thought the conflict presented a serious problem, as the following statements suggest:

> I've seen conflict, for example, where members feel the organizers are having too much to say. And that has been the cause of a group of people splitting off who felt they should have a bigger say and that the organizers should be sitting back from it. Usually if there is a dispute, the members speak up and the organizer adjusts. They don't realize they're intruding too much. The organizers I've been with have universally been well-meaning and if you tend to say, "Well, look, I think we should do it this way instead of that," they'll be reasonable to listen. And if they don't think they should back off, they'll convince you or if you think you're right, they'll do it.

> Since I am the head person within the community ... the membership will call on me and make a complaint. Then I'll go directly to the organizer. And it's always worked out.

One might reasonably expect members to be somewhat reticent to discuss serious dissatisfaction with a researcher, but the evidence does not suggest that conflict is a serious problem.

Thus, the interviewees strongly endorsed the quality of democratic decision making in Boston ACORN. They claim that members play the most important role in the process and that organizers do not dominate the organization. While several of the respondents expressed mild dissatisfaction, this was outweighed by the enthusiasm of the others.

Members' Political Views

In order to assess the value of purposive incentives in ACORN and understand the potential conflicts that such incentives may create, we must determine and analyze the members' political views. This provides a way of assessing ACORN's success in creating a progressive political movement.

The interview included two relevant sets of questions. The first was a set of opinion questions on issues that are generally associated with a progressive political agenda. The second asked for the interviewees' ideological views and party allegiances.

The opinion questions covered topics from nuclear energy to a guaranteed annual income. Two of the questions were about issues ACORN has been actively involved with: housing and health care. Several broader social questions (on the Equal Rights Amendment and abortion) were also included. Finally, foreign policy and arms spending questions determined how they fit in the political understandings of the members. The complete text of the questions is found in Appendix I.

The responses to issues questions fell into three patterns of consensus and dissensus among the respondents. Table 5-3 shows a distribution of the members' responses dividing the issues into categories based on the level of agreement among them. Three patterns are discernable in the interviewees' responses: "strong consensus," "dissensus," and "dissensus with many undecided." The questions on ERA, health care, and housing elicited strong agreement among nearly all the respondents with only one "don't know" response among them. This suggests, first of all, that the members' involvement in ACORN campaigns on the health care and housing issues have established the saliency of those issues and shaped their attitudes. Also, since all but one of the respondents were women, the support for ERA suggests a high level of solidarity among them on this issue.

There was strong dissensus on the issues of guaranteed annual income and abortion. Again, the paucity of "don't know" responses indicates strong and well-developed opinions. The "strongly agree" and "strongly disagree" responses show significant disagreement being expressed on these issues. Moreover, the dissent from the progressive agenda is clear. The dissensus on the social issue of abortion demonstrates social conservatism among the interviewees in this study and the

94

TABLE 5-3

MEMBERS' ISSUE STANDS

	Str. Agree	Agree	Dis- Agree	Str. Disag.	Don't Know	Total
Strong consensus						
Pass ERA	8	9	1	0	1	19
Free medical care for needy	8	11	0	0	0	19
Free housing for needy	8	10	1	0	0	19
Dissensus						
Provide guaranteed annual income	4	4	7	1	3	19
Govt. should pay for abortions for needy	2	5	8	2	2	19
Women have a right to abortions	3	9	5	1	1	19
Dissensus with many undecided						
Should socialize essential public services	0	5	7	1	6	19
Should stop nuclear power	3	8	4	0	4	19
Cease U.S. involvement in Latin America	2	6	4	1	6	19
Should continue arms buildup	1	7	5	1	5	19

membership of ACORN. The question on the guaranteed annual income also presents problems regarding government benefit programs for low-income people. Thus, this group of issues labeled "dissensus" reveals problems that progressive political organizers must deal with when they work with this constituency.

The third category had fewer responses in the "strongly agree" and "strongly disagree" categories and many more "don't know" responses. These issues, vital to many activists on the progressive left, are not salient to the interviewees, although the organizers cited issues such as American involvement in Latin America and the Reagan Administration arms buildup as critical to their original involvement in political organizing.

The question on socializing essential public services such as electric companies struck a responsive chord among political activists who have been involved in many utility rates conflicts. Certainly, the utility issue has not been framed in quite such a manner, but long-time members surely have had opportunities to acquaint themselves with issues related to public service corporations. Hence, this third category included some important issues that have not been addressed directly by ACORN but are important to the progressive left agenda.

The Organizers' and Members' Views Compared

The contrast between the organizers' and members' views can be demonstrated by comparing their responses to these issues. The four organizers were unanimous in their strong agreement to ERA, free medical care for the needy, and a woman's right to an abortion. The only other responses were "don't know" (3), "agree" (6), and two "undecided" responses. Thus, the organizers adhere consistently and intensely to the progressive agenda contained in the issue questions.

Another way to compare the political views of the members and organizers is to look at their responses to the questions on ideology and party identification. Table 5-4 compares the ideologies of the two groups:

TABLE 5-4

IDEOLOGY OF MEMBERS AND ORGANIZERS

	Very Liberal	Liberal	Mod- erate	Conserv- vative	Very Cons.	Don't Know
Members	3	5	8	1	1	1
Organizers	2	1	0	0	0	1

The members show a tendency toward the middle, hence, the eight "moderate" responses. Two members described themselves as "conservative." The organizers, on the other hand, readily referred to themselves as "liberal" or "very liberal." One refused to classify himself, since he felt his ideology did not fit the categories offered.

Party identification showed differences between the members and organizers as well. Table 5-5 presents these differences:

TABLE 5-5

PARTY IDENTIFICATION OF MEMBERS AND ORGANIZERS

	Strong Democ.	Democ.	Indep.	Repub.	Strong Repub.	Don't Know
Members	6	7	4	1	1	0
Organizers	0	1	2	0	0	1

The organizers have either weak or no allegiances to party while some members have strong allegiances. This shows further differences in political views and perspective.

ACORN Activism and Political Views

Since organizers operate under the assumption that ACORN activism will change the way members think about politics, it is useful to compare levels and longevity of activism with political views on the issue questions in the interview. I multiplied the respondents' length of membership in ACORN by the number of activities in which they have engaged to create an Activity Scale -- a measure of ACORN activism. I calculated levels of progressive ideology by assigning a value of two to "strongly agree" responses, one to "agree," zero to "don't know," minus one to "disagree," and minus two for "strongly disagree." (Scores for the arms buildup responses are reversed.) This creates a Progressive Index -- an estimate of the conformity of the respondents' responses to a left progressive agenda. Table 5-6 provides the scores of all the respondents on these indices. The respondents' scores on the Activity Scale fall into three categories: high, medium and low. The respondents with the high scores (36-72) are all long-time members who have engaged in most of the activities cited in the interview. The middle category (16-30) includes members who have been in ACORN for a moderate length of time (two years) or have been in longer but have not participated in a wide variety of activities. The respondents with low Activity Scores (0-15) have all been in ACORN for less than a year. The different categories correspond to distinct differences among the interviewees' experiences. It is useful, therefore, to compare the three categories according to ideology, party identification, and Progressive Index to determine if there are significant differences.

Ideology responses show some significant differences between

TABLE 5-6

ACTIVITY SCORES (Years in ACORN x Activities)
v. POLITICAL VIEWS

Activity Score	Years Member	Activities	Ideology	Party ID	Progressive Index
High:					
72	4	18	L	D	12
56	4	14	VC	D	7
45	3	15	VL	I	10
44	4	11	M	I	8
42	3	14	L	SD	4
40	4	10	M	D	6
39	3	13	VL	SD	5
36	4	9	L	SD	10
Medium:					
30	5	6	M	R	2
28	4	7	M	D	2
26	2	13	L	SD	3
22	2	11	M	D	4
18	2	9	M	SD	-1
16	4	4	C	R	1
Low:					
8-2/3	2/3	13	VL	D	7
2	1/2	4	M	SD	1
1-1/2	1/2	3	L	I	3
1	1/6	5	DK	D	5
3/4	3/4	1	M	D	7

the high activity group and the others. High scores identify with liberalism more clearly; to a lesser degree, they express allegiance to the Democratic Party. What most clearly distinguishes them from the others, however, is the Progressive Index. The average index for the high activity group was 7.75, with scores ranging from four to twelve. The medium activity group average was 1.83 and the range was from minus one to four, while the low activity group averaged 4.6 and ranged from one to seven.

The evidence from this data shows that intensity and duration of ACORN activism may have had an impact on the

TABLE 5-7

ACTIVITY SCORES v. IDEOLOGY AND PARTY ID

POLITICAL VIEWS OF RESPONDENTS WITH HIGH ACTIVITY SCORES (N=8)

Ideology		Party ID	
Very conservative	1	Strong Republican	0
Conservative	0	Republican	0
Moderate	2	Independent	2
Liberal	3	Democrat	3
Very liberal	2	Strong Democrat	3

POLITICAL VIEWS OF RESPONDENTS WITH MEDIUM ACTIVITY SCORES (N=6)

Ideology		Party ID	
Very conservative	0	Strong Republican	0
Conservative	1	Republican	2
Moderate	4	Independent	0
Liberal	1	Democrat	2
Very liberal	0	Strong Democrat	2

POLITICAL VIEWS OF RESPONDENTS WITH LOW ACTIVITY SCORES (N=5)

Ideology*		Party ID	
Very conservative	0	Strong Republican	0
Conservative	0	Republican	0
Moderate	2	Independent	1
Liberal	1	Democrat	3
Very liberal	1	Strong Democrat	1

---

*1 "Don't Know"

---

interviewees' political views. It is noteworthy, also, that the low activity group exceeds the medium group in several of the categories. This suggests that Boston ACORN has attracted some individuals with progressive views from among its targeted constituency and has not had to rely solely on ACORN participation to instill those ideas.

The differences among the interviewees raise some questions about the way that purposive incentives operate in ACORN. The members who fell into the middle category -- for example, who had been long-time members yet were quite conservative -- raise the question of what the members perceive as ACORN's goals. In other words, why do they contribute to an organization that promotes a program designed to foster progressive leftist change in American politics when they do not share those values? The entire question of the relationship between ACORN activism and ideology surely merits further study. The next section raises the questions of what members think ACORN is trying to accomplish and how likely it is to succeed. These questions are equally important, for what is the purpose of contributing when the chances of success are small?

Organizational Goals

Members were asked about ACORN's national and local goals. While some members responded with specific goals, such as rent control or more low- and moderate-income housing, others spoke in more general terms about creating a power base:

> We hope to gain more political power through the neighborhood structure. And that's by getting more people involved in political issues. Say, for instance ... the majority of people in the neighborhood don't know who their representatives are. So that's one of our goals we would like to give the people, so at least they know who their representative is and make the representative accountable to the neighborhoods.

Those who responded with specific issues were asked to be as thorough as possible in order to obtain a numerical count of issues and be able to better compare answers. One interviewee could not cite any goals of Boston ACORN, four cited fewer than three, eight cited between four and seven, and five either cited more than seven or gave responses that reflected a broader, more involved understanding of Boston ACORN's goals such as the one quoted above.

When members were asked about ACORN's national goals, they gave similar responses but with lower frequencies. Six stated they did not know of any national goals, some adding they were not at all familiar with the national organization. Five cited four or fewer goals, two cited a moderate number of goals, and six either gave a long list of goals or made broader statements such as:

> All the things we've been trying to work:

> unity, between low- and moderate-income people,
> and that way we can crack poverty and all the
> hardships poor people have, education-wise,
> foodwise, even, in some cases, things like that.

or:

> Better conditions of the poor. That's the way I
> see it. They want change, they want things
> people are entitled to. That's the way I see
> it.

It is clear from the higher incidence of "Don't Knows" that the members were more familiar with ACORN's local than national activities.

A further sense of identification with the goals of the organization was tested when members were asked if and why they thought ACORN was successful in attaining its goals. The positive responses followed three themes: unity, hard work, and the development of political clout. Negative responses centered on the difficulties of motivating members to participate and the recalcitrance of powerholders in the political system. Thirteen of the nineteen responded that they felt ACORN was quite successful, one said it was unsuccessful, and three were ambivalent. Two did not have an opinion of ACORN's degree of success.

Positive responses to ACORN's political success were unreserved in their praise. The ones who praised its unity made comments such as:

> It's an organization. It's a community. It's
> working with different issues. You work with
> housing, there's a number of organizations that
> only work on one issue, they only work on
> housing. But if you've got a health problem,
> that's not their problem. That makes a big
> difference in how ACORN works and how other
> organizations work.
>
> Togetherness they have been. In dealing with
> people. They even brought people together that
> wouldn't be together.
>
> We fight hard. Like I said, it's a handful of
> people, but when a handful of people band

together, it's a whole community. All we do is
just band together.

We're always just like a big happy family.
When they come in and we all go out to a
meeting they all come back here to my house and
sit down and eat together. They get tired out
in the street, that's [pointing to her couch]
they bed. We're just like a big happy family.
There's no prejudice with us.

Further evidence of identification with the organization and its
goals was shown by statements regarding the hard work invested in
ACORN's success:

Communications among the people and the
members, and hard work. Very hard work.

Because they are very active. And they started
off with nothing they've been working up and I
think they're doing good.

Finally, those who cited ACORN's political power as a reason
for its success displayed a degree of pride and identification,
though less intensely than the statements of the kind made above.

Because sometimes when you call the people
[e.g., city officials] up, they think you're
another ACORN group. They have heard about
ACORN. There really is some recognition
there. I think they're successful where they
need to be successful -- the people that's
responsible for the things we want. They seem
to know that we are here. We're not an
invisible person ... as we were without the
organization.

In the different campaigns that we have
launched, we have gained more recognition, more
clout and everybody's really acknowledged in
the goals that we've had how really successful
we are ...

For one thing, they have the backing and
support of the people. And then, I notice that
when we have to go to city officials or state
officials, they kind of fear ACORN for some

reason. I guess they're aware that we're a group that has a lot of power and strength behind us. When we send them a letter or make a phone call or go to their office for an action, nine times out of ten, they respond quickly. Because they fear if they don't, ACORN is going to go to the newspapers and blow it up. So they get results because I think they really fear they're playing around with a powerful organization.

Among the respondents who thought ACORN was successful, therefore, the three themes of unity, hard work and power were clearly articulated.

Not all of the respondents were as sanguine about ACORN's level of success. Doubts about its performance center on the difficulty of developing a powerful organization of low- and moderate-income people:

You're dealing with people who are inexperienced in politics, and naturally, they make mistakes, sometimes. People join and drop out. Ultimately, when you consider we began with people who were just unemployed sharecroppers out in Arkansas, and we're in twenty-six, twenty-seven states now, and in three or four cities we're having some effect in the elections we're very successful.

We've got a long way to go yet. Well, mostly, I know not all members can be like me, but I haven't been attending the meetings and keeping up with what's going on, but the rest of them don't do that either. It's going to pot. If the younger people stick with the meetings and keep up with what's going on they can do much better.

If we don't get the members to actively push for all these issues then we're not gonna get anywhere. I think that Boston is a little slow compared to some of the other places.

Hence, several of the members recognize that low- and moderate-income people lack skills and experience and -- as much of the scholarly literature attests -- are not strongly motivated toward sustained participation in political organizations.

Finally, one respondent emphasized the resistance that ACORN faces in working on its goals:

> At City Hall they more or less ignore our issues, they don't see the importance. They're more interested in the business district, in putting more money in that.

The final set of questions, designed to determine the members' commitment to ACORN's goals, asks what they would do if ACORN departed from its multi-issue agenda and became a single-issue organization. The researcher chose the single issue each interviewee had previously stated was most important. Many of the responses asserted strongly that ACORN's goal was power or that remedying the problems of all of the members was the primary goal:

> I think all goals are important. I can't say that one is more important than the other. No matter how small, they're all important. Ten blocks away might be an issue concerning street lights that ACORN's dealt with. To those families over there that's a major importance to them because of safety in their area -- to walk and there's no streetlights and it's dark and there's crime, people are afraid. So that's important to them. I think every issue is important.

> The most important, of course, is jobs. And the health. And housing. All of it is the most important. Trying to separate is kind of hard, because they're all like connected. You've got to have health to work, you've got to have a house to live in when you come home from work, so they all connect, so you can't say, "The most important."

> The important goal is power. People are getting some sense of control of their own lives, rather than simply following the drift of obeying orders from some civil servant. They can organize and get some input for a little bit of control over their day-to-day lives.

The same sentiments were expressed when they considered the question of transforming ACORN into a single-issue organization:

> I wouldn't feel too great about that because that's what makes us an organization above all other organizations. Most of the other organizations just have one thing that they can deal with; they can't deal with other issues. I think that's a handicap. I would not feel good about it at all.
>
> If you just start focusing in on just housing, on just jobs, then you're coming away from where you said you were. And I wouldn't like to see them do that at all. I like the way they're set up, I like the way they work, I've been happy working with them, and if there were any changes geared that way, in other words, coming in from other organizations, focusing on just main issues, I wouldn't like to see that. Because ACORN has many goals, and the main goal is to help the low- and moderate-income person.

The response indicated a high degree of confidence in the organization and satisfaction with the multi-issue format. Further, many of them articulated one of ACORN's central themes: the necessity of the multi-issue strategy for building power and realistically addressing the needs of the low- and moderate-income constituency.

Tactics

Given the organizers' views on tactics and their impact on the members and the kinds of effects they are designed to create, it is useful to examine the members' views on those tactics, especially confrontive tactics. It is critical to the success of the organization that the members are positively disposed to the tactics in which they are engaging.

Discussion of tactical questions with the members took two paths: questions as to (1) the kinds of groups the members feel are good allies, and (2) the kinds of tactics that are effective in achieving the organization's goals. The first set is designed to determine how the members feel about other organizations; the second set is intended to probe the experiences members have had participating in these activities, discover their preferences, and determine their readiness to engage in the various tactics.

Finally, interviewees were asked if they prefer confrontational or bargaining tactics. This gave members an opportunity to expand on their preferences and cite which features they think are most important about the organization's tactics: respectability, hostility, drama, camaraderie, dignity, and so on.

Table 5-8 gives the results on questions about coalition partners the members feel are the most effective to work with:

TABLE 5-8

COALITION PARTNERS

	Excellent	Good	Fair	Poor	Don't Know
Unions	4-1/2	9-1/2	0	0	5
Churches	2-1/2	5	4-1/2	1	5
Peace groups	2	4	4	0	9
Politicians	1	9	3	0	6
Community organizations	2	6	4	0	7
Students	1	7	1	0	10

It shows little difference between organizations. The only important difference seems to be between unions and other groups; labor is the only category without "fair" or "poor" responses and it leads in "excellent" and "good" responses.

Aside from that, members seem to be rather charitable in their assessments. Only one "poor" was chosen, and every choice got at least one "excellent." Thus, the responses do not seem to indicate a distaste for other organizations for whatever reason. The sympathy for unions perhaps suggests some class solidarity.

Table 5-9 also shows few differences in responses about tactical effectiveness. The two tactics that received the highest number of "very effective" responses were actions in a public office and inviting opponents to attend ACORN meetings. Both of these hold honored places in the standard notions of what is democratic in American politics. Certainly, one must be able to protest to public officials for redress of grievances, and one should give an opponent an opportunity to be heard. The two "don't knows" given to inviting opponents to meetings also seem to indicate that members are familiar with this tactic, which is

TABLE 5-9

MEMBERS PERCEPTIONS OF EFFECTIVENESS OF TACTICS

Type/Tactic	Effectiveness Ratings				
	Very Effect.	Effect.	Somewhat Effec.	Not Effec.	Didn't Know
ELECTORAL:					
endorse candidate for election	5	11	2	0	1
campaign for an endorsed candidate	6	10	0	0	3
elect ACORN member to office	5	5	1	2	6
CONVENTIONAL:					
attend public hearing on issue	7	5	1	0	6
have political supporter speak at an ACORN meeting	5	10	1	0	3
conduct a referendum campaign	3	0	0	0	10
CONFRONTIVE:					
conduct an action in a public place	8	7	1	0	3
conduct an action in a private place	3	7	1	1	7
demonstrate on the street	3	9	1	0	6
have political opponent speak at an ACORN meeting	9	7	0	1	2
block traffic on a street	4	6	1	4	4

widely used by ACORN groups.

The same can be said about endorsing candidates, an activity that the Boston chapter of ACORN has performed frequently in the last two years. Conversely, ten "don't knows" for referenda campaigns show a clear unfamiliarity with this political tactic. Finally, the four "not effective" responses given to blocking streets seem to indicate a distaste for this activity among the interviewees. The difficulty of executing it and the risks involved could explain this figure.

The interviewees' support for confrontation was not strong.
The categories of responses include: (1) confrontation is the
most effective; (2) bargaining works better; and (3) one must
choose the style that fits the given situation. People who
preferred confrontation did so for a variety of reasons:

> ... Everyone knows and sees and hears about
> it. And lots of those things are embarrassing
> to the public -- ... they don't want to be
> embarrassed. It's more public ... people know
> more what's going on. We've been out marching
> and dealing and people they had no idea what
> was happening. The more people know, the more
> effective it is.

> Bargaining can be a long, drawn-out thing. To
> do it directly is much more impressive to the
> people [the target of the action].

> It's a shock to the system. To shake you up.
> Wake up somebody. Somebody said once they
> didn't think there was a racial problem in
> Boston. They needed confronting. Because if
> they can't see a problem, something wrong
> somewhere. They probably have never been
> confronted with the real issues. Sometimes
> it's more effective.

> [confrontational?] Always. You have to meet
> the person face-to-face. In order to get
> whatever you want done. You cannot, I never
> like an aide writing me back for anything. The
> mayor, for example, "the Mayor said ..."
> There's nothing like meeting the Mayor
> face-to-face. I'd rather hear it from the
> Mayor's mouth. I want to hear it from the
> Senator's mouth. I want to hear it from the
> President of the bank's mouth. I don't want to
> hear it from his secretary.

It is clear that the members who chose confrontational tactics
feel that opportunities to address the individual responsible for
solving a problem and express grievances directly are both more
effective and more satisfying. Moreover, their public nature
draws attention to the issue and increases their moral leverage.
Finally, their responses indicate that they feel confrontation
conveys more information to the target about the gravity of a

situation and can be more powerful in moving the target.

Not all of the respondents share this affection for confrontational tactics. Several felt they hurt more than helped:

> I thought they carry too many members when they went down to talk with city officials. It was to get in to talk with city officials. It was hard to get in to talk with them, but if they'd had two strong mens or a woman and a man, to ... sit down and talk to them they might have talked to them. We couldn't get to Mayor White, none of them. We just couldn't get to them, they just wouldn't come out.

> ... We went there with papers demanding and as a result, we didn't get it. I don't think it was a good tactic to use.

Others seemed more pragmatic and suggested that the tactic should fit the situation; one should bargain when the other party seems prepared to bargain in good faith and confront when they do not:

> They all work. It's according to the people, but the end is the same because you never start out confronting them. We always start out calling them and talking to them. And if that gets what we want, that's all we do. We only confront them when they will not talk. When they tell you they're going to a meeting and they will not give you an appointment to come in and talk to them, the response you get from whom you are approaching determines what procedure you're gonna follow.

Thus, some of the answers express desire to confront, others, a reluctance. Still others feel it is a matter of expediency; whatever will succeed in a given situation.

Conclusion

The members' responses provide a great deal of information on their experiences in, and perceptions of, ACORN as a political organization. They help answer some of the critical questions regarding political organizing of low-income people in American politics: why they join political organizations, what role they play in the organizations, and how participation affects their views on public policy issues. The final chapter will discuss the members' and organizers' insights and perceptions in the context of my experiences and the prevailing theories of political organizing.

C H A P T E R   V I

CONCLUSION

When I completed my fieldwork in New Orleans, organizing a neighborhood in a low- and moderate-income area, I experienced two overwhelming feelings: satisfaction and wonder. The satisfaction came from looking over the neighborhood and seeing stop signs erected and vacant lots cleared at the request of the newly-formed group, within a few months. My sense of wonder stemmed from the creation of a dynamic and complex system of organizational interaction through a series of seemingly mundane activities.

Residents of the neighborhood were aware of the problems that existed. Over the years, they had attempted to form community groups to deal with them. At no time, however, had so much been accomplished to improve the quality of life in so short a time.

Moreover, the improvements came as a result of a group effort by community residents. This laid the groundwork for continued improvement by and for the community; several years later, an open drainage canal that bordered two sides of the neighborhood was covered over at a cost of several million dollars, attesting to the continuing impact of the ACORN group -- and adding to my sense of wonder.

I had no significant political experience prior to the fieldwork. Had I gone into the neighborhood and begun speaking to the residents about the need for improved traffic safety or covering the drainage canal, there is no reason to believe that the organization would have succeeded in creating the degree of change that actually occurred. Despite many hours in the hot New Orleans summer sun, I did not sense that I had done anything dramatic, difficult, or brilliant. Rather, I simply followed the ACORN Organizing Model relatively closely, maintaining the procedures and schedules it prescribed. The experience was very much like following a recipe in cooking and creating a beautiful dish, without having made anything similar to it or understanding the theory behind the process. The process unfolded, the members joined, the "wins" were achieved, and the organization succeeded. It was a process that has occurred many times in ACORN's history -- a new organizer without political skills or experience signs on and receives on-the-job training in the first neighborhood organizing drive.

This experience goes to the heart of this study. The satisfaction and wonder I experienced is the source of my curiosity and desire to understand political organizations -- particularly ACORN. This study leads me to believe that the two vital ingredients in ACORN's success are the organizer/entrepreneur and the organizing strategy. The political science literature has not given adequate attention to them. Both of these are implied in much of the literature, but this study has sought to expose them more fully and recognize their importance in understanding political organizations.

In addition to those ingredients, this study also brings out some other important elements that contributed to my unexpected feelings of satisfaction and wonder. First, the satisfaction was not what I would have predicted. My ideological leanings were toward the left and clearly attuned to ACORN rhetoric. I did not expect that satisfaction would come from stop signs and mowed vacant lots. Nor did I expect that these successes would be so critical as part of ACORN's larger goal of building a power base for low- and moderate-income people.

Second, I did not realize that an individual organizer was so critical to the success of an organizing drive. Neighborhood residents made major contributions to the organization's ultimate success, but I, as the organizer, initiated the process, coordinated the work, maintained the schedule of events, and orchestrated interests, issues, energies and goals. Without my initiative to enlist members, either personally or with the help of members, virtually no one would have joined. Few, if any, joined without being asked directly to pay dues and take part. Some only joined after being approached several times.

Most of those who participated did so in response to frequent and repeated requests to take part in a number of specific activities, from meetings to actions at City Hall. The requests, however, were not appeals to specific self-interest but were part of the organization's routine activities as I presented them. They did not know if these activities were routine for ACORN or similar political organizations. They relied on my judgment and on their sense of the legitimacy of the organization.

CONCLUSION

The ACORN Organizing Model was, and is, a source of valuable
knowledge -- both theoretical and practical -- regarding
political organizations that can be tapped by political science.
While I had studied political science as a student, often
focusing on organizational theory and the concerns of low-income
Americans, I was not familiar with the principles of low-income
organizing contained in the Organizing Model. Indeed, the
process taught by the model and the Head Organizer who trained me
contained little that I could recognize as rational calculation
or thorough organizational planning, yet the resulting
organization had a significant impact on the neighborhood and its
residents. This study has sought to frame the satisfaction and
wonder I experienced into a better understanding of the process
-- one that strengthens the reader's and my understanding of
political organizations in general.

The data from the interviews provide valuable findings.
They are not **major** departures from the conventional wisdom on the
membership decision and subsequent formation of political
organizations. The analysis of incentives and the application of
the concept of organizing strategy do not revise thinking on
political organizations. Rather, they confirm some notions and
refine others in the process of reorganizing the concepts in a
systematic fashion.

This study offers two levels of analysis and two
perspectives from which to view these data: (1) from the
individual level, and (2) from the organizational level. The
perspectives are those of both the constituent and the
organizer/entrepreneur. We are able, therefore, to learn both
what the entrepreneur is trying to do and how the constituent
perceives those efforts. Therefore, we can evaluate the theories
of group formation and membership decision in light of each
other. The conclusions we can draw from the data are not new,
but possess an added degree of validity owing to their origin.

Theories of Group Formation Revisited

Before evaluating the results of the interviews and their
implications for the major theories of group formation, let us
review the contending theories. Essentially, they fall into two
categories, plus a synthesis of these. These categories are
generally referred to as the sociological theory, argued by David
Truman,[1] and the economic theory, first proposed by Mancur
Olson.[2]

Truman's sociological theory claims that stress on a group

that shares interests in the political system by virtue of, for
example, common socio-economic status, will cause members of that
group to increase mutual interaction and promote the formation of
groups to protect their common interests. But the economic
theory argues that group formation is usually not rational;
members will probably not recoup the costs of group formation
through group activities. Hence, the people who are under stress
calculate that their decision to join the organization to promote
their interests will cost them more than they will get in
return. Thus, the focus of the study becomes the trade-off of
contributions required against incentives offered.

Syntheses of the two theories, especially Terry Moe's,[3]
argue for a more complex process of group formation. Moe focuses
on the relationship between the constituent and the
entrepreneur: how the constituent calculates tradeoffs of
contributions and incentives in the complexity of the actual
political process. He notes, for example, that the entrepreneur
is strongly motivated to manipulate the information so that the
constituent is more likely to decide to join. This notion of
"bounded rationality" is clearly more like a real interaction
between an organizer/entrepreneur and a constituent than either
of the previous theories. Moe's categorization of incentives
also includes all of the varieties that James Q. Wilson
identifies:[4] material, solidary, and purposive. With this
broader categorization, we can appreciate fully the complexity of
the political interaction.

The ACORN Theory of Group Formation

The ACORN model of organizing, in essence, is a theory of
group formation and maintenance -- one that is constantly tested
by practice. In particular, the organizing drive described in
the model should be considered as a prediction of the results one
should expect if an organizer follows the model and attempts to
organize a neighborhood.

It is my experience that following the organizing drive
"recipe" works quite well, despite the inexperience of the
organizer. Naturally, experience and acquired skills improve the
quality and efficiency of organizing work. Yet, the model, based
on an incentive system of collective material benefits, anger,
and constituent desire to join forces with others in the
neighborhood, is sufficient to recruit approximately ten per cent
of a targeted low- and moderate-income neighborhood. This has
been borne out by hundreds of successful drives, many conducted
by very inexperienced individuals. The technique is based on

organizing principles which can be applied to constituents of similar economic background to organize successful ACORN groups anywhere in the country.

The organizers of Boston ACORN speak in terms that are nearly identical to those of the ACORN Model -- which they all study and apply in their organizing. They claim, for example, that self-interest is necessary to motivate constituents to join an ACORN group. The organizers recognize that the self-interest they describe may be somewhat broader than the individual, i.e., it frequently involves the quality of life for the neighborhood at large and may not specifically affect every individual member. Their claim to produce deliverables works on this broader self-interest, which is calculated in a manner very much like Olson's analysis of tradeoffs and decision making. The organizers also cite purposive incentives such as the opportunity to build an effective community group and take action on what one organizer said were "aspects of peoples' lives that, before, they didn't know they had any control over." They also admit to using anger -- getting constituents "oiled up." Thus the Boston ACORN organizers perceive -- and expect -- that the bases of the ACORN Model are valid both to predict phenomena and analyze the relationship between the organization and the constituents.

Group Formation Theories of ACORN Members

The members' views on political organizing differed from the ACORN Model and the organizers' views only in emphasis. In fact, when they discussed their own recruiting techniques, the members' responses were almost identical to the organizers'. The most important factor that influenced members to join was the opportunity to help the community. While similar to a self-interest theory, this appeal shifts the emphasis to a community service and away from individual benefits. The category of service to the poor is an even greater shift of emphasis away from self-interest.

The most direct articulation of the pursuit of self-interest is the desire to work on specific issues such as health care or housing, and the desire for self-improvement expressed by some of the members interviewed. The question, "How do you recruit new members?" most clearly resembled the organizers' responses on how they persuade people to join. Hence, when asked what induces people to join, members' answers will shift emphasis, depending on whether the person is referring to him- or herself or another. Neither the literature nor the data from this study provide any insights into this phenomenon.

This study is useful in considering the debate between the sociological and the economic approaches to the membership decision. The members and the organizers of Boston ACORN agree that the ACORN Model is fundamentally sound: that some notion of self-interest combined with anger, a desire to serve the community, and purposive incentives are effective in motivating people to join. This conclusion supports the economic model of political organizing.

Truman's contention that increased interaction among peers causes group formation fails to take into account the potent impact of face-to-face contact between organizer and member. One organizer stated the point clearly from a strategic point of view:

> I think that's something that we really pride ourselves on is that that's how we recruit our members ... by knocking on people's doors. And that's why, in a lot of ways, our base is made up of a lot of people that aren't necessarily gonna get themselves involved politically or organizationally in something else.

Thus, the claim that increased interaction alone leads to group formation is inadequate, especially in reference to low-income people -- who are nearly always under some kind of social or economic stress.

When one attempts to analyze group formation (as opposed to the individual's membership decision), it is clear that this study strongly substantiates Robert H. Salisbury's argument[5] for the importance of the organizer/entrepreneur in group formation. My experiences and observations, the literature on and by ACORN, and the comments of both members and organizers all bear this out. In ACORN, the organizer/entrepreneur is an essential feature of group formation. An understanding of that role is required for an adequate analysis of grassroots-based political organizations.

Both organizers and members responded positively to questions that implied the concepts that constitute the economic model. Therefore, this study substantiates that model as well. Moreover, their articulation of the organization's goals supports expansion of incentives beyond purely economic ones, despite Wilson's argument that low-income people require greater economic incentives than higher income people do. But perhaps the most compelling refutation of the sociological model is the fact that

116

the actions of the professional organizers are what is critical
to the creation of political organizations. From either the
organizer's or the member's perspective, organizations are
created and members recruited by devising and applying an
appropriate organizing strategy.

Maintenance of Membership

The basic question of what keeps members in ACORN -- or
organizations in general -- is closely related to the membership
decision. This is even more true for a voluntary activist
organization of low-income people. Unlike organizations that
require only dues, voluntary activist organizations continually
ask their members to provide resources that the organization
requires. Hence, members ask themselves, in the model of the
economic analysis, "is it in my self-interest to engage
repeatedly in this organization's activities?" Moreover, as
Richard C. Rich argues,[6] the nature of the voluntary
organization offers the exit option each time the organization
requests resources. Again, while this feature of the
organization lowers the costs of membership for the constituent,
it raises the cost of organizational maintenance.

Given the nature of ACORN as a voluntary activist
organization, David Knoke and James R. Wood's analysis of social
control,[7] or commitment, is applicable to this question. They
argue that commitment grows from three features of an
organization: purposive incentives, member participation, and
professional legitimacy. The interviews treated these topics in
several ways.

Purposive incentives involve either goals or ideology.
Hence, the interview questions that dealt with ACORN's goals and
those that probed the members' perceptions of policy issues are
both pertinent. It is clear that members did not articulate
ACORN's goals effectively, especially its national goals. Only
the members who had attended national conventions had a good
sense of the national goals or of the nature of the national
organization. Several suggested that issues like stop signs were
important for the national organization.

According to Gary Delgado, realization of the members' lack
of understanding of larger issues in ACORN is what led to the
People's Platform in 1980. The process of widespread input into
the planks of the platform was specifically designed to integrate
the national organization by articulating national goals and
involving members in the creation. The responses of the

interviewees in this study show that this strategy did not touch many ACORN members.

Ideological commitments of the members were neither uniform nor strong. The only issues on which there was solid agreement were ERA, housing, and health care. While it is important to note that the consensus on housing and health care issues very likely resulted from ACORN's efforts, it is also important to recognize deep splits on issues like abortion and, potentially, government income supplement programs. These splits suggest limits on issues on which ACORN can effectively mobilize its membership.

Interviewee responses to the questions relating to ideology present more insights into this problem. Several of the members stated that ACORN's goal as an organization is to create power for low- and moderate-income people. This kind of organizational purpose seems sufficient as a purposive incentive, however vague. Nevertheless, in apparent contradiction to Knoke and Wood's thesis, these interviews suggest that members are willing to continue to contribute to ACORN despite a lack of commitment to goals they cannot articulate and an ideology that is not particularly salient to them.

The question of participation as a means of enlisting the continued allegiance of ACORN members raises a related question: How much control do members have over the decision making process in ACORN? Knoke and Wood argue the necessity for involvement of members in the decision making process, but this raises some serious problems for the organization. To operate an organization of low-income, inexperienced activists effectively, an organizer -- not the members -- must at times make important decisions.

This dilemma has troubled ACORN greatly. The professional role of the ACORN organizer is to promote maximum participation in the decision making process and the formal structure of the organization is designed to ensure member controls via the board of directors. However, ACORN is faced with the classic problem of all such organizations: the desire of the professional staff to control the decision making process in order to ensure the success of the organization.

The ACORN Model and the responses of the members and organizers in the interviews all suggest that the organization generally succeeds in eliciting members' participation and allowing them at least a veto over the organization's decisions.

Moreover, many of both types of participants argued strongly that the members have a profound control over the decision making process. One organizer, for example, claimed that issues never arise solely from the organizing staff but only from the inputs of the members via the doorknocking process.

Delgado, a long-time ACORN organizer, also found that when asked, ACORN members cited organizers' roles only as providing "technical assistance and/or resource development."[9] He goes on to say that

> Within ACORN, as within most large community organizations, organizers do in fact call the shots in terms of organizational direction; the organization has in fact become a staff oligarchy. That development is understandable: with greater size and complexity, increased specialization, and departmentalization, it is simply not possible for all members to possess enough of the relevant information for informed decision making; therefore, communications increasingly flow from the top down.[10]

Without genuine involvement of the members, it is not possible to change their perceptions so they see themselves as politically efficacious and identify with the organization. Moe argues that this point pertains particularly to voluntary membership organizations with mixed incentive systems:

> [A] participatory context ... is significantly different from what we have found for material associations. It is more open, in the sense that any individual can be highly motivated to engage in various activities, regardless of his economic position. It is also more conducive to socialization effects, in which individuals can be changed in important ways as a result of their participation. And, notably, it enhances the prospect for member involvement in decision making, especially through purposive bases for contributing and participating ...[11]

While Delgado refers only to decisions of the national organization, participation in that decision making process is only possible for a rather small group. Thus, at that level, very few members can use participation opportunities to develop their commitment to the organization.

On the other hand, local chapters of ACORN do involve the members, both on the board and in local groups. Judging by the interviews, however, organizers frequently are the ones who translate the constituents' issues into campaigns, strategies, and tactics. Thus, even at that level, membership control of the organization -- and the commitment that that engenders -- is limited.

There are virtually no limits, however, on the member participation in functions such as member recruitment, leadership roles at the lower levels, fundraising, actions, and so on. Organizers use every opportunity to involve members in these activities -- not only to lighten their workload, but to build involvement and commitment among the members. The members' listings of activities in which they engaged attest to the organizers' success in this effort. Further, the members' increased identification with the progressive agenda results from their long-standing and intense involvement with ACORN. This indicates that Knoke and Wood's thesis can be brought to bear at a level of participation below that of the decision maker.

The third part of Knoke and Wood's social control concept is legitimacy of the professionals. This raises the question of the membership's faith in the integrity and abilities of the organizers. The lack of conflict between members and organizers is one component of professional legitimacy within ACORN. The members also defer to the organizers' decisions regarding tactics and issues. Moreover, member descriptions of their initial reluctance to engage in certain tactics and their subsequent participation in them attests to their faith in the organizers' judgment. Interviewees also reported a willingness to change campaigns on which they were working, without particular distress or misgivings. Hence, when the organizers suggest that a particular tactic or issue is vital to the organization, the members go along with that decision.

Thus, in applying Knoke and Wood's formula for organizational commitment, the interviews suggest that the degree of commitment to purposive incentives and opportunities to participate in decision making are limited. However, other kinds of participation are extensive, and professional legitimacy is high.

This combination has been effective for those interviewed: nearly all were very enthusiastic about ACORN and many contributed their time and energy generously. While some of those have strong commitment to ACORN's goals and are involved in important decisions, others seem to be active due to the organizers' persistence combined with tangible results and opportunities to serve their community. Thus, the goal of creating an organization of involved, informed, and progressive low- and moderate-income people is being achieved -- but only with the support of those members who do not develop a progressive world view.

Organizers

The professional organizer is poorly understood in American politics. Recent studies of political organizations have given the organizer a prominent place in political science theory. This has begun bringing that role into proper focus: as creator and motivator of many political organizations, especially voluntary membership organizations.

This study began by examining some important questions about political organizations in light of participants' perceptions. These perceptions have led back to fundamental questions of organizational dynamics that can only be appreciated if one understands the role of the organizer. Moe argued forcefully, for example, that limited rationality is the basis for the membership decision: this prompts organizers to "bend" the realities of group membership in a way that will persuade people to join.[12] Yet he does not fully develop the concept as it applies to continued participation by members. Knoke and Wood stress the importance of social control for the organizer's success but do not pursue the extent to which the organizer devises and implements the organizing strategy.

The lack of attention to the organizer's central role is probably a function of the kind of organization studied. Moe concentrated on economic organizations; Knoke and Wood examined middle class cause organizations. Both types rely on organizers in different ways. Economic groups prefer to leave the operation of the group entirely to professionals. Middle-class groups can and do call on a reservoir of experienced and educated members to serve in planning and organizing roles.

Boston ACORN, however, recruits a constituency of inexperienced, poorly educated people. Unlike small businesspeople and professionals, for example, they have few organized means of expressing political interests. The impetus for organizing the ACORN constituency comes from outside the constituency. A consciously devised plan is articulated and applied by professionals, who have a vague but compelling goal for their constituents. As Delgado points out, the continued operation of ACORN requires more skill, time and energy than the membership can provide. Hence, the organizers have a more demanding role in the organization than might otherwise be the case.

Understanding the organizer's role in an organization like ACORN yields practical as well as scholarly insights. For anyone interested in creating an organization with a constituency similar to ACORN's, the conceptual groundwork had been laid by ACORN in the Organizing Model and the incentive system, i.e., the strategy that has proven effective over the years for ACORN. For students of American politics, this approach to political organizations provides useful insights about the members; they are generally not highly ideological but are committed to the organization and its goals. Both practitioner and scholar should recognize the significant but limited role of the organizer. Organizational dynamics, including the goal of member empowerment, limit the organizers' ability to control or manipulate their constituents.

The Organizers' Relationship to the Members

Given the connections among ideology, socioeconomic and cultural background, and goals for involvement with ACORN, a special kind of relationship must be established between the organizers and members. This is particularly true in light of the importance of professional legitimacy for many of the members' continued involvement in ACORN. This relationship centers on two basic ideas: the exit option and professionalism. Both of these rein in the organizers' notions of what issues and tactics ACORN should pursue. Thus, when organizers suggest issues or tactics that fit their views on politics but not their members', they limit themselves by their professional ideals, and the members limit them by exercising the exit option. Thus, if the members perceive that an issue, candidate, or tactic is not desirable, the organizers are unlikely to persuade members to participate in those activities. In an important sense, then, the exit option keeps the organizers honest, preventing the ideological differences between organizers and members from causing serious problems in ACORN.

However, the exit option is not the only control on the organizers. They also share a professional ethos; they feel an ethical obligation as professionals to promote maximum member participation in order to gain increased allegiance, improved skills, increased resources, greater turnout and enthusiasm, and democratic control of the organization. One purposive incentive that drives the organizers is the desire to play a democratizing role in the political system to give low- and moderate-income Americans a genuine opportunity to influence the political system without being controlled by organizers.

In the case of the ACORN organizers, the ethos of member participation contains within it several other elements as well. First, it is part of the democratic ethos that has shaped reformist and radical components of American political culture. This is profoundly different from the role of organizer/entrepreneurs in traditional economic organizations. The latter perceive their role as professionals, akin to lawyers: hence, they provide the incentives, operate the organization, and lobby, yet have no desire to train their constituents to become more effective citizens. Lawyers have no desire to teach their clients the law or improve their ability to promote their interests via legal means. Traditional organizer/entrepreneurs operate similarly, keeping information costs high so that their clients will continue to require their services.

While ACORN's organizing ethos does not prevent ACORN organizers from controlling many of the decisions of the organization, it constrains centralization of power. Second, the democratic ethos the organizers articulate is as much a part of the organizing strategy as the organizing drive itself. It has proven to be an effective way to recruit and maintain membership, as is evident in the almost mythical quality it has attained among members and organizers. The organizers also recount instances when it has benefited their organizing efforts; this further attests to its utility.

Thus, the strains within ACORN created by cross purposes of organizers and members are, to some extent, controlled by other features of the organizations: professionalism and voluntarism. The ethic of the organizer to maximize member control and combines with the organization's voluntary nature to provide clear constraints against organizer abuse of power within the organization.

Ideology as Incentive

The treatment of ideology in ACORN is particularly important, given the responses of members and organizers to policy questions. There are clear differences between members and organizers, and the way these are handled is critical to the success of the organization. The motives of the organizers for taking a low-pay, high-demand job are strongly centered on the desire to change society and pursue left-wing internationalist goals. There is no indication that the members share these goals.

Some of the members have adopted the rhetoric of ACORN -- power for low-income people, "Taking What's Ours!" and so on, but there are clear differences of ideological perspective in specific policy areas, ideological self-identification, and party identification. The organizers avoid conflict or erosion of trust by using vague language and populist sentiments rather than Marxist ideology or leftist rhetoric. This allows a degree of latitude for the organizers to pursue policy goals that are anti-corporate without being explicitly leftist; it provides a broad canopy for both white and black constituents; and it excludes as few people as possible given the possible range of political views that could be attracted to such as organization. Thus, ACORN's approach to ideology serves organizational ends of unity between disparate groups whose energies and commitment are both engendered and endangered by ideology.

The interviews suggest that ACORN's approach has been effective. The members regularly defer to the organizers' views on what the organization should do. The level of conflict between the two groups is low. Moreover, both members and organizers agree that the existing conflicts have nothing to do with their views on politics, but rather center on organizers' failure to consult the members. The members believe the organization should be run by them and, when it is not, they make it an issue. Members and organizers agree on how ACORN should be run and act accordingly.

The closest thing to ideological conflict is the question of the desirable level of confrontational tactics. As the organizers note, they sometimes have difficulty persuading members to confront their targets. The difference surfaces not on the issue or the choice of target, but on the degree of conflict that is appropriate for the situation. Hence, the agreement on issues and broad goals is large enough to appeal to all the participants in the organization; conflict only arises around the intensity necessary to pursue these issues and goals.

CONCLUSION

Confrontation as Ideology

The issue of confrontive tactics has several dimensions: demands on the membership, tactical effectiveness, and organizational identity, both internal and external. In addition, confrontive tactics are part and parcel of ACORN's vague ideology.

Confrontive tactics increase the demands on the members. They recognize immediately that more is being asked of them when they carry signs and raise hell than when they quietly attend a meeting. More energy is required; more risks are involved; there is greater chance of arrest; they will not be welcomed. Participants in prospective confrontations commonly have doubts about the propriety of rowdiness, and the justification for disrespect expressed toward the target. Mike Silver notes that members are "sometimes ... most put off not by fear of arrest or violence but by confusion, uncertainty, and a sense of helplessness in unknown situations."[13] Mary Kay Harrity, writing about members of the Bridgeport, Connecticut chapter of ACORN, noted that the members

> seem somewhat hesitant about some of the more dramatic actions ACORN has used to make its point, like a candlelight march in Colorado that ended with demands for changes in utility rates being nailed to wooden planks ... or claiming "squatters' rights" in abandoned Philadelphia homes ...[14]

Some members perceive a cost in social status or respectability.

Confrontational tactics, according to several writers on organizing, are the bread-and-butter of low-income organizing. The low-income constituency has rather limited resources. If their resources are forcefully and directly applied, the argument goes, they will be more effective:

> It isn't conflict for its own sake, but to create incentives for the other side to negotiate in good faith, to reach an agreement that takes care of a problem. The point is, to have genuine bargaining, first we have to show the other side we have power.[15]

Frequently, the mass confrontation is the most powerful weapon available to the ACORN group. Thus, as Lee Staples suggests, it

125

is wise for local ACORN groups to reserve that tactic for a point in an issue campaign in which other, less costly and difficult, tactics have proven ineffective.[16]

The importance of confrontational tactics extends beyond their ability to move others to respond to their demands into questions of the organization's identity in some important ways. First, they separate ACORN from its opponents: utility companies, many of the local politicians, bureaucrats, and others who are in a position to satisfy or deny their demands. They also unify ACORN internally, building identification among the membership:

> The best victories will be those achieved through direct action on the part of large numbers of people. Campaigns featuring a high level of direct action enable the leaders and members to experience their own collective power. The organization lesson is, We won because lots of us stuck together and fought like hell.[17]

Taking demands to the extreme and engaging in highly expressive protest creates strong ties among the members and shared feelings of great intensity, especially if the tactics pay off in a victory. The memory of the activity and the expression of solidarity builds into the organization a sense of unity and identity.

A tactic at the 1982 Democratic National Mid-Term Convention illustrates this point well. While ACORN members demonstrated in the street for low- and moderate-income representation in the nominating process, a group of ACORN members sneaked into the hotel where a fund-raising luncheon was being held with some large donors to the Democratic Party. The ACORN members worked their way into the hotel via the coffee shop, the gift shop, and other avenues -- singly and in small groups that would not attract attention. When they arrived at the service door of the luncheon hall, they burst suddenly into the hall, chanting and demonstrating. This and other tactics that require bravado and make noise all serve to increase the solidary benefits of the organization and increase the members' shared identity with ACORN.

In light of the above discussion of ACORN's approach to ideology, the role of confrontation as ideology becomes clear. While avoiding divisive issues such as abortion, ACORN has defined itself in terms of its opponents and its internal solidarity. Also, when ACORN assumes a policy position, it expresses that position in terms of action and style rather than specific points of argument. Delgado explains how ACORN used this technique to express its views on housing issues:

> While it is clear that tactical militancy does not necessarily relate to or translate into a progressive ideology, ACORN's recently launched multistate squatting efforts, in which low-income people in twelve cities are taking over abandoned houses, certainly demonstrates the organization's <u>attitude</u> toward private property and translates the attitude into action.[18]

The use of squatting actions gave the membership an opportunity to express its views without having to articulate complex arguments or adopt ideological stances. The actions were sufficient to create and pursue purposive goals.

This approach, ACORN organizers hope, will avoid internal division over ideological issues and alienation of potential members and allies. Perhaps more important, ACORN organizers avoid expending energies on deciding the "correct" stance to take on issues. Rather, as Rathke has stated, the way to organize is to appeal to constituents' concerns, not philosophical issues:

> Our membership aren't out there in the clouds somewhere saying this is the way the world should look in 100 years. Our philosophy is very closely related to our membership's daily life experience. There's no ideology that instructs what we do. People make decisions and start moving.[19]

Hence, developing an ideology is not a part of effective organizing according to ACORN organizers. Confrontation is an important means by which ACORN can maintain purposive incentives while keeping goals as vague as possible.

The ACORN Organizing Strategy and the Majority Constituency

From its inception, ACORN's goal has been to organize a majority constituency of the lower 70% of the income scale. ACORN's history and the history of similar organizations indicate formidable problems involved in achieving this goal. While

ACORN's organizing model is capable of creating organizations in either low-, or moderate-, or mixed-income neighborhoods, difficulties have arisen when ACORN has pursued broader objectives than neighborhood improvement issues. Moreover, the confrontive tactics have created divisions among the low- and moderate-income groups.

The unifying feature that Rathke defines for the constituency ACORN targets is that they are not participants in the important decisions that shape their lives. He claims that the important decisions in American political and economic life are made by large corporations and the very wealthy. His goal for ACORN has always been to unite low-income and moderate-income Americans into a unified organization that can vie successfully with the decision makers in American society. Uniting these two groups, however, requires that they can be convinced of their mutual interests. That has not always been the case.

This problem of unifying the targeted constituency has arisen in a variety of ways, including disagreement over tactics, dominance by moderate-income members, and conflict over issues. In ACORN's history, each of these issues has been a problem that the leaders and organizers have grappled with in an effort to keep ACORN moving towards its organizational goal of organizing the majority constituency. Both the problems and the means of addressing them provide insights into the nature of political organizations and the organizing strategy they employ.

As noted above, confrontive tactics have not been popular among all of the ACORN members. This plays a role in the internal divisions within ACORN as well. Low-income members more readily adopt confrontive tactics to promote their interests with the limited resources they possess. If they need jobs from construction firms building in central city areas, they cannot pressure the job providers behind the scenes. Rather, they must disrupt the job site or go to City Hall with pickets in order to get results.

This situation is quite different for moderate-income people. Cloward and Piven, writing in 1979 about the differences in community organizing among the two groups, distinguished between low-income organizing and "citizen action" organizing. They note that citizen action organizing

> produces a membership with a marked reluctance to go beyond conventional political channels. Citizen action consists mostly of meetings,

hearings, research memoranda, petitions, lobbying, and referenda. "The impulse not to demonstrate," says Mark Splain [an ACORN organizer], "but to call the alderman because they <u>know</u> the alderman!"[20]

Moderate-income members who are originally attracted to ACORN for community improvement are often repelled by confrontational tactics. In 1979, Pearl Ford, a board member, resigned from ACORN because of differences over tactics.

The tactics sounded good at first. They come into a neighborhood and ask if you need stop lights and your trash picked up. The next thing you know they get you involved in storming City Hall and other things that I don't approve of.[21]

Conversely, low-income members would not respond to the kinds of tactics that moderate-income members prefer. The low-key style of politics denies them the opportunity to participate effectively using the resources at their disposal -- anger, disruption, and enthusiasm. Moreover, the issues that they must address -- jobs, housing, medical care -- are often controlled at a higher social level than city services like streets, vacant lots, garbage removal, and stop signs. Thus, there is a distinct difference between the tactics that are usable for the two different income ranges within ACORN's constituency.

Writers on community organizing have noted a tendency for moderate-income members to dominate community organizations. Michael Walzer argues that

[T]heirs is not, by any means, a "poor people's movement." They have not done very well among welfare recipients, tenants of public housing projects, unemployed men and women. The groups they are able to form and sustain mostly involve (relatively small numbers of) better-off workers and members of the low-to-middle class. And the politics of these groups is clearly reformist; the neighborhood alliances often take on a kind of "community uplift" character. Self-help against crime, the defense of old residential areas, improvement of local services, beautification; these are the goals, to which the organizers too must stand committed.[22]

Cloward and Piven recognize this same phenomenon. They argue that it results from three causes: (1) the search for anti-corporate issues via consumerism; (2) the ease of organizing moderate-income neighborhoods; and (3) the dependence of many neighborhood organizations on canvassing as a source of income.[23]

In an effort to forge an anti-corporate stand that will attract members, particularly from the upper end of their constituency, consumer issues have been effective and attractive. Also, moderate-income residents are less intimidated by political activity and organizational membership. Finally, the canvassing method of fundraising -- in which canvassers go into upper-income neighborhoods and request donations -- has restrained some groups.

> It is reasonable to surmise that the growing financial dependence of these groups on canvassing contributes to their emphasis on popular consumer issues and on conventional politics. "If our canvassers tell us that an issue or tactic won't sell in the suburbs," one organizer said, "we give it a second thought."[24]

Cloward and Piven, however, excepted ACORN from the organizations that had adopted this course. They attribute this difference to "ACORN's organizers [who] have a commitment that guides their organizing and orients them to low-income people. Much of this direction probably comes from Wade Rathke, ACORN's chief organizer, whose professionalism is tempered by a strong sense of mission."[25]

In the late 1970s, Rathke and other members of the national ACORN staff recognized their members' upward drift in income and adopted a course of action to involve more low-income people in the organization. They pursued organizing drives of the unemployed in several cities and worked to organize low-income labor groups such as household workers in New Orleans and home health care workers in Boston. Thus, ACORN has avoided overdependence on moderate-income members.

The history of ACORN has, in fact, followed that pattern of development: pursuing different ends of the income scale at different times. Madeleine Adamson and Seth Borgos, both former

ACORN professional staff, describe the process of alternating between the two ends of the income spectrum of ACORN's targeted constituency:

> For ACORN, the squatters campaign was the culmination of a five-year quest to recover the audacity and militance of its welfare rights origins -- qualities which had been diluted in the pursuit of a majority constituency. More recently, ACORN has moved closer to the contemporary mainstream, organizing a national coalition of labor, church, minority, and peace groups to challenge the policies of President Ronald Reagan. Such periodic swings are characteristic of ACORN's evolutionary pattern: a continual dialectic between low- and moderate-income, mobilization and organization, expansion and consolidation, militance and accommodation.[26]

Thus, ACORN has sought a balance between the desire to include low-income constituents and the need for the resources that moderate-income constituents can provide. The historical evidence, however, provides clear arguments for the difficulties of unifying ACORN's targeted constituency. As Adamson and Borgos claim, ACORN has been forced to "drift towards one or another segment of their constituenc[y] or to oscillate between them, never really mobilizing the whole."[27]

The problem with issues within ACORN clearly demonstrates this dilemma. Historically, the lower-income ACORN members have pursued more progressive issue stands than the moderate-income membership. This is very clear from the events surrounding the drafting of the ACORN People's Platform. Delgado reports that the difference between the income groups was reflected in the longevity of the groups represented:

> The older ACORN groups were dominated by low-income people who had fought for welfare and Medicaid reform; the newer ones were more likely to comprise homeowners and blue-collar workers. The difference was especially prevalent in the ACORN affiliates in California, North Carolina, and Georgia, where the lowest-income elements were the senior citizens' groups.[28]

Some of the Arkansas representatives were people who had been a part of the original drives to organize welfare recipients in Little Rock and who were disposed to pursue clearly progressive issues such as the guaranteed annual income:

> It was on this issue that the tenuous coalition of low- and moderate-income people on which the organization is built was most seriously challenged. Advocates of the plank (mostly black and low-income members) argued that all families were entitled to a basic income, health care, and housing; opponents of the plank (the most vociferous of whom were also black but more moderate-income) argued for income based on employment.[29]

Boston ACORN members' responses to the same question showed a lack of understanding of the issues -- and certainly no unified support. Thus, the problem of creating and maintaining the majority constituency manifests itself in terms of low-income tactical militance, the attractiveness of the moderate-income group's more conservative approach and role as organization-sustainers, and the conflict that arises between the two groups over issues within the organization.

Nevertheless, the necessity to unify the two groups is clear. If one is attempting to oppose the political and economic elite in American politics, it is not possible to do it with only part of the low- and moderate-income constituency.

Saul Alinsky recognized that fact late in his career as an organizer. He began his career in 1939 in the Back of the Yards area of Chicago, one of the most desolate slums in America at the time. By the early 1970s, his pursuit of a middle-class constituency that would promote radical or anti-corporate goals led him to devise the proxy strategy. He enlisted middle-class corporate shareholders and those who are capable of influencing institutions that hold shares (such as universities) to raise issues at shareholders' meetings of large corporations and disrupt their proceedings.

> I'm directing all my efforts today to organizing the middle class, because that's the arena where the future of this country will be decided. And I'm convinced that once the middle class recognizes its real enemy -- the megacorporations that control the country and

> pull the strings on puppets like Nixon and
> Connally -- it will mobilize as one of the most
> effective instruments for social change this
> country has ever known. And once mobilized, it
> will be natural for it to seek out allies among
> the other disenfranchised -- blacks, chicanos,
> poor whites.[30]

Alinsky did not live to pursue this strategy to its end.
Nevertheless, ACORN's experience suggests that the assumptions he
made about the natural inclination of the middle class to seek
allies among low-income and minorities are questionable.

However, an observer of ACORN politics must recognize that
Rathke and the other top leaders and organizers in ACORN are
working toward long-term goals. As Rathke has stated, his goal
is power for the majority constituency over the fundamental
decisions in the American political and economic system. Because
the goal is so far-reaching, he argues that it is not possible to
predict what form that power will take. Moreover, it is not
possible to predict under what circumstances that assumption of
power might occur. It is conceivable that an extraordinary turn
of events, a crisis of great proportions like the Great
Depression, could provide unity for the low- and moderate-income
groups.

In order to take full advantage of the situation, ACORN must
be a fully operating organization. Thus, if there were an
economic disaster, the middle class would be alienated from the
upper class and share common issues with lower-income Americans;
this would create the opportunity for the larger goal of ACORN
organizing. Until that time, ACORN organizing continues in its
present strategy of fluctuating between the desire to be radical
and the necessity for organizational survival.

Organizing Strategy and Political Analysis

The notion of organizing strategy was originally conceived
by political organizers to facilitate organizing by replicating
organizational characteristics in many places at once. It is
also effective in analyzing political organizations. In this
case study of Boston ACORN, the use of the concept of organizing
strategy has directed the research at the important features of
the organization and illuminated their interaction in the
participants' functioning.

Perhaps the most important contribution of organizing

strategy to political analysis is the stress it places on the strategic nature of political organizing. Because it compares political organizing to product marketing, it illuminates the kind of thinking that is required for the organization to succeed. The organizers, as entrepreneurs, must decide on and mobilize a constituency. They must also decide what resources the organization requires from the constituents in order for it to succeed. Finally, they must determine what organizational structure will best serve the group's goals.

The concept of organizing strategy requires that the analyst see all of the above decisions as part of a whole. For example, the decision to use neighborhood improvement as an incentive to initiate members into ACORN requires that the structure of the group be based within neighborhoods; the desire of ACORN organizers to pursue progressive political issues prompts them to organize a low-income constituency that will agree to those issues in an enthusiastic way; the need for a broad-based constituency requires that organizers demand a maximum amount of participation by the membership.

Finally, organizing strategy helps to explain some of the wonder and satisfaction I experienced after organizing an ACORN neighborhood. It makes the connection between mundane items like stop signs and great issues like housing and democratic control of corporations. It helps to explain how an organization can bend and shape the goals of both members and organizers to coincide in a mutual effort. It shows how well an organization can develop the political skills of people who have historically both avoided and been excluded from political participation. It explains how the apparently undramatic actions of organizers and constituents in neighborhoods across the country have the potential for dramatic impact on the lives of many low- and moderate-income people and, conceivably, the American political system.

Notes to Chapter VI

[1]David B. Truman, The Governmental Process (New York: Alfred A. Knopf, 1962).

[2]Mancur Olson, The Logic of Collective Action (Cambridge, MA: Harvard Univ. Press, 1965).

[3]Terry M. Moe, The Organization of Interests (Chicago: Univ. of Chicago Press, 1980).

CONCLUSION

[4]James Q. Wilson, _Political Organizations_ (New York: Basic Books, Inc., 1973).

[5]Robert Salisbury, "An Exchange Theory of Interest Groups," _Midwest Journal of Political Science_ 13 (February, 1969), pp. 1-32.

[6]Richard C. Rich, "A Political-Economy Approach to the Study of Neighborhood Organizations," _American Journal of Political Science_ 4 (Nov., 1980), pp. 559-591.

[7]David Knoke and James R. Wood, _Organized for Action_ (New Brunswick, NJ: Rutgers Univ. Press, 1981), pp. 12-13.

[8]Gary Delgado, _Organizing the Movement_ (Philadelphia: Temple Univ. Press, 1986), p. 137.

[9]Ibid., p. 185.

[10]Ibid.

[11]Moe, p. 121.

[12]Ibid., p. 18.

[13]Mike Silver, "Before and After the Action," in _Roots to Power_, ed. Lee Staples (Westport, CT: Greenwood Press, Inc., 1984), p. 161.

[14]Mary Kay Harrity, "ACORN: Putting Down Roots in Bridgeport," _Fairfield Advocate_ 2, no. 13 (Nov. 14, 1979), p. 7.

[15]Silver, p. 160.

[16]Staples, p. 97.

[17]Ibid., p. 65.

[18]Delgado, pp. 156-157.

[19]Ibid., pp. 190-191.

[20]Richard A. Cloward and Frances Fox Piven, "Who Should Be Organized? 'Citizen action' vs. 'Jobs and Justice'," _Working Papers_ (May/June 1979), p. 40.

[21]Delgado, p. 117.

[22]Michael Walzer, "The Pastoral Retreat of the New Left," _Dissent_ (Fall, 1979), p. 407.

[23]Cloward and Piven, pp. 38-40.

[24]Ibid., p. 40.

[25]Ibid., p. 38.

[26]Madeleine Adamson and Seth Borgos, _This Mighty Dream_ (Boston: Routledge and Kegan Paul, 1984), p. 125.

[27]Ibid., p. 128.

[28]Delgado, p. 141.

[29]Ibid.

[30]Eric Norden, "_Playboy_ Interview: Saul Alinsky," _Playboy_, 9, no. 3 (March, 1972), p. 177.

INTERVIEW SCHEDULES

Member Interview

I. I want to start with some questions about how you and
    others originally get involved in ACORN.

    (1) How long have you been an ACORN member?

    (2) Were you involved in politics before you joined ACORN?
        Tell me about that.

    (3) Why did you join ACORN? What attracted you to ACORN?

    (4) What does it mean to you now to be an ACORN member?
        What do you get out of it?

    (5) How has the experience of being in ACORN differed from
        your original expectations?

    (6) When you talk to someone who is thinking of becoming
        involved in ACORN, what reasons do you give them to
        join?

II. Now, I want to talk to you about your activities and
    involvement in ACORN.

    (1) Do you belong to other organizations? Are you active
        in them? Hold office in them? How many hours a week
        do you spend on them?

    (2) How many hours a week do you spend on ACORN?

    (3) Which of the following have you participated in?

        ___ Attended a national ACORN convention
        ___ Organized or worked for an ACORN fundraiser
        ___ Held an office in ACORN
        ___ Signed a letter of support for ACORN
        ___ Recruited new members

137

___ Spoken at public hearing, like the City Council,
as an ACORN representative
___ Marched in an ACORN action
___ Led an ACORN action
___ Canvassed your neighborhood -- "got out on the
doors"
___ Held meetings in your home
___ Flyered a neighborhood
___ Talked to people about ACORN in a public place like
a store
___ Chaired an ACORN meeting
___ Made phone calls for an ACORN meeting or action
___ Worked on an election or issue campaign
___ Helped provide direct member services
___ Attended a national action or training workshop
___ Served on the ACORN Political Action Committee

III. The next set of questions deals with ACORN's goals and your
feelings about them.

(1) Can you list ACORN's political goals here in Boston and
in your neighborhood?

(2) What are ACORN's national goals?

(3) Has ACORN been successful with those issues?
If YES, what do you think makes ACORN successful?
If NO, why do you think ACORN has not been successful?

(4) Which goal is the most important? Why?

(5) Are any of these goals not very important? Why?

(6) Do you think ACORN should pursue more issues or less?
Why?

(7) If ACORN changed the way it operates -- say, it only
dealt with one goal ["most important goal" above] --
how would you feel about that?

IV. I'd like to learn some things about ACORN's direct member
services. Things that only ACORN members can get, like the
newsletter.

(1) What direct member services does Boston ACORN offer?
Do you participate?

(2) If ACORN stopped providing direct member services and only worked on political goals, would you stay in ACORN?

(3) If ACORN stopped working on political goals and only gave the direct member services, would you stay in ACORN?

V. Now I want to talk to you about your views on some important political issues.

(1) First, which of the following best describes you?

    (a) ___ very liberal
        ___ liberal
        ___ moderate
        ___ conservative
        ___ very conservative

    (b) ___ strong Democrat
        ___ weak Democrat
        ___ Independent
        ___ weak Republican
        ___ strong Republican

(2) Now tell me if you agree or disagree with the following statements. Please respond: "Agree strongly," "Agree," "Disagree Strongly," or "I Don't Know."

    (a) The federal government should provide a guaranteed income to all citizens.
    (b) The government should take over industries that provide public services, like the utility companies.
    (c) It is important to pass the Equal Rights Amendment.
    (d) The federal government should provide free medical care to all needy citizens.
    (e) The construction and use of nuclear power plants should be stopped.
    (f) Government should build or subsidize housing for those in need.
    (g) The federal government should help low-income people pay for abortions.
    (h) Abortions are a constitutional right.
    (i) The U.S. should not get involved in Latin American affairs.
    (j) The U.S. should continue to build up its military

139

defense.

(3) Is ACORN working on the right issues? Do they ignore issues you think should be addressed?

VI. I'm interested in how ACORN makes decisions about issues and tactics.

(1) Who makes the important decisions in ACORN? How is it done?

(2) Are you involved in making important decisions?

(3) If your ACORN group took a stand on an issue that you could not agree with, what would you do?

(4) If your ACORN group endorsed a candidate you could not support, what would you do?

(5) If your ACORN group used a tactic you could not participate in -- picketed a church gathering, for example -- what would you do?

(6) Do conflicts ever arise over important issues within ACORN? If so, how are they worked out?

(7) Are there ever conflicts between organizers and members? What causes them? How are they resolved?

VII. I'd like to know some things about the way ACORN pursues its political goals. Use the choices on the sheet to answer these questions: "Very effective," "Effective," "Somewhat effective," "Not effective," or "Don't Know."

(1) Of the following groups, tell me what you think of them as partners in coalitions with ACORN:
____ unions
____ church groups
____ peace groups
____ elected officials
____ other community organizations
____ student groups
____ any I left out?

(2) Of the following tactics, tell me what you think of them as a means of achieving ACORN's goals.
____ ACORN members running for office

_____ demonstrating in public offices; the Mayor's, for example
_____ demonstrating in private offices, like a corporate building
_____ demonstrating in the street
_____ speaking in public hearings
_____ inviting opponents to speak at ACORN meetings
_____ inviting supporters to speak at ACORN meetings
_____ blocking streets
_____ endorsing candidates
_____ campaigning for endorsed candidates
_____ running referenda campaigns
_____ anything I left out?

(3) Which do you think are more effective: confrontational tactics or bargaining tactics?

VIII. Finally, I'd like to discuss with you your feelings about your impact on politics. Use the choices on the page to answer this group of questions: "Very Likely," "Likely," "Not Likely," "Very Unlikely," or "Don't Know."

(1) If the Mayor and City Council were considering an ordinance that would hurt your neighborhood, could you help prevent it from passing?

(2) If the state legislature and Governor were considering a law that you considered unfair to you or your interests, could you help prevent it from passing?

(3) If the President and Congress were considering a law that you opposed, could you help prevent it from passing?

(4) If you took an issue to a government office to express your views -- on a budget question or a housing program, for example -- would you be treated as well as anyone else?

(5) If you tried to explain your views on an issue to city officials, would they take your point of view into serious consideration?

(6) Do you think: (a) city politicians in Boston do--
                  (b) Mass. state politicians do--
                  (c) politicians in Washington do--
an excellent job?

a good job?
a fair job?
a poor job?
don't know.

PERSONAL DATA:

Race:
___ Asian
___ Black
___ Hispanic
___ White
___ Other

Sex:
___ Male
___ Female

Age:
___ 18-25
___ 26-31
___ 32-40
___ 41-50
___ 51-60
___ 61 or over

Education:
___ Completed 6th grade
___ Completed 9th grade
___ Completed high school
___ Some college
___ Completed college
___ Graduate school

Household Income:
___ under $8,000
___ $8,100-$9,999
___ $10,000-$14,999
___ $15,000-$19,999
___ $20,000-$29,999
___ $30,000 or over

Number in household:
___ one
___ two
___ 3-4
___ 5-8
___ 9 or more

Occupation _____

Spouse's occupation _____

Organizer Interview

I. I'd like to start with a discussion of why people get
    involved in ACORN.

    (1) How long have you been an organizer?

    (2) Why did you become an ACORN organizer?

    (3) Has ACORN organizing been what you expected it to be?
        Explain.

    (4) What do you get out of ACORN organizing?

(5) What attracts members to ACORN?

(6) When recruiting new members, what kind of appeal do you make?

(7) What keeps members in ACORN?

(8) When recruiting new organizers, what kind of appeal do you make?

(9) Do you think members' goals for ACORN change over time?

(10) Do you think organizers' goals for ACORN change over time?

II. Next, I'd like to discuss peoples' level of involvement with ACORN.

(1) What kinds of members become most committed to ACORN?

(2) Do you think level of involvement enhances commitment?

(3) Do you think organizers are subject to those dynamics?

(4) What about your involvement -- have you held staff or supervisory positions?

(5) How long do you expect to keep on with ACORN? Why? Other plans?

III. I'd like to talk about ACORN's goals and its ability to achieve them.

(1) What are ACORN's political goals locally/statewide/ nationally?

(2) Is ACORN achieving those goals? Explain.

(3) Should ACORN tackle more or fewer issues?

(4) Do you think ACORN's goals should be broader or narrower?

(5) Are members flexible about changes in goals? Is one type more or less flexible than others?

IV. I need to learn some things about ACORN's selective

incentives.

(1) What selective incentives does Boston ACORN offer its members?

(2) What is the participation rate?

(3) Do selective incentives improve recruiting or membership?

(4) What purposes do they serve?

(5) Are selective incentive participants more or less goal-oriented than non participants?

V. I'd like to discuss your general views on political issues. What are your politics?

(1) First, which of the following best describes you?

    (a) ___ very liberal
       ___ liberal
       ___ moderate
       ___ conservative
       ___ very conservative

    (b) ___ strong Democrat
       ___ weak Democrat
       ___ Independent
       ___ weak Republican
       ___ strong Republican

(2) Now tell me if you agree or disagree with the following statements. Please respond: "Agree strongly," "Agree," "Disagree Strongly," or "I Don't Know."

    (a) The federal government should provide a guaranteed income to all citizens.
    (b) The government should take over industries that provide public services, like the utility companies.
    (c) It is important to pass the Equal Rights Amendment.
    (d) The federal government should provide free medical care to all needy citizens.
    (e) The construction and use of nuclear power plants should be stopped.
    (f) Government should build or subsidize housing for

those in need.

(g) The federal government should help low-income people pay for abortions.

(h) Abortions are a constitutional right.

(i) The U.S. should not get involved in Latin American affairs.

(j) The U.S. should continue to build up its military defense.

(3) Is ACORN working on the right issues? Do they ignore issues you think should be addressed?

VI. I'm interested in how ACORN makes decisions about issues and tactics.

(1) Who makes the important decisions in ACORN? How?

(2) If ACORN took a stand on an issue that you disagreed with, what would you do?

(3) If ACORN endorsed a candidate you could not support, what would you do?

(4) If ACORN used a tactic you disagreed with, what would you do?

(5) Do conflicts ever arise between members and organizers? between members and members? between organizers and organizers? If so, how are they resolved? What is their source?

VII. I'd like to discuss some of the ways ACORN exercises its power tactically.

(1) Tell me what you think of the following groups as coalition partners. Are they "Very Effective," "Effective," "Somewhat Effective," "Very Ineffective," or "Don't Know"?
____ unions
____ church groups
____ peace groups
____ elected officials
____ other community organizations
____ student groups
____ any I left out?

(2) Tell me what you think of the following tactics. Are

145

they "Very Effective," "Effective," "Somewhat Effective," "Very Ineffective," or "Don't Know"?
___ ACORN members running for office
___ demonstrating in public offices
___ demonstrating in private offices
___ demonstrating in the street
___ speaking in public hearings
___ inviting opponents to speak at ACORN meetings
___ inviting supporters to speak at ACORN meetings
___ blocking streets
___ endorsing candidates
___ campaigning for endorsed candidates
___ running referenda campaigns
___ anything I left out?

(3) Do you have any philosophical commitments to specific tactics or types of tactics?

(4) What is the importance of confrontational tactics? Do they have advantages over cooperative coalition-building?

(5) Do you find that some tactics are more popular among members than others?

VIII. Finally, I'd like to discuss the members' efficacy and confidence.

(1) How do you build efficacy among your members? How effective is it?

(2) What kinds of members respond best to efficacy-building efforts?

(3) How do political officeholders and bureaucrats respond to ACORN members? Do they take them seriously? Why or why not?

BIBLIOGRAPHY

Books

Adamson, Madeleine and Seth Borgos. This Mighty Dream: Social Protest Movements in the United States. Boston, Routledge and Kegan Paul, 1984.

Alinsky, Saul. Reveille for Radicals. New York, Vintage Books, 1969.

Bailis, Lawrence Neil. Bread or Justice: Grassroots Organizing in the Welfare Rights Movement. Lexington, Massachusetts, D.C. Heath and Company, 1974.

Barnard, Chester I. The Functions of the Executive. Cambridge, Massachusetts, Harvard University Press, 1938.

Bentley, Arthur F. The Process of Government. Cambridge, Massachusetts, The Belknap Press, 1967.

Botsch, Robert. We Shall Not Overcome. Chapel Hill, North Carolina, University of North Carolina Press, 1981.

Dahl, Robert. A Preface to Democratic Theory. New Haven, Yale University Press, 1956.

_____. After the Revolution? New Haven, Yale University Press, 1975.

Delgado, Gary. Organizing the Movement: The Roots and Growth of ACORN. Philadelphia, Temple University Press, 1986.

Fainstein, Norman I. and Susan S. Fainstein. Urban Political Movements: The Search for Power by Minority Groups in American Cities. Englewood Cliffs, New Jersey, Prentice-Hall, Inc., 1974.

Gaventa, John. Power and Powerlessness: Quiescence and Rebellion in an Appalachian Valley. Urbana, Illinois, University of Illinois Press, 1980.

Goodwyn, Lawrence. The Populist Moment. New York, Oxford
University Press, 1978.

Herring, Pendleton. Group Representation Before Congress.
Baltimore, Johns Hopkins University Press, 1929.

Hofstadter, Richard. Anti-Intellectualism in American Life. New
York, Alfred A. Knopf, 1963.

Kahn, Si. Organizing: A Guide for Grassroots Leaders. New
York, McGraw-Hill Book Company, 1982.

Knoke, David and James R. Wood. Organized for Action:
Commitment in Voluntary Associations. New Brunswick, New
Jersey, Rutgers University Press, 1981.

Lancourt, Joan E. Confront or Concede: The Alinsky Citizen-
Action Organizations. Lexington, Massachusetts, D.C. Heath
and Company, 1979.

Lukes, Steven. Power. Cambridge, U.K., Cambridge University
Press, 1970.

McKenna, George. American Populism. New York, G.P. Putnam's
Sons, 1974.

Milbrath, Lester W. Political Participation. Chicago: Rand
McNally and Company, 1965.

Mills, C. Wright. The Power Elite. New York, Oxford University
Press, 1959.

Moe, Terry. The Organization of Interests: Incentives and the
Internal Dynamics of Political Interest Groups. Chicago,
University of Chicago Press, 1980.

Olson, Mancur. The Logic of Collective Action: Public Goods and
the Theory of Groups. Cambridge, Massachusetts, Harvard
University Press, 1977.

Pateman, Carole. Participation and Democratic Theory.
Cambridge, U.K., Cambridge University Press, 1979.

Schattschneider, E.E. Politics, Pressures, and the Tariff. New
York, Prentice-Hall, Inc., 1935.

Staples, Lee. Roots to Power: A Manual for Grassroots

BIBLIOGRAPHY

Organizing. Westport, Connecticut, Greenwood Press, Inc.,
1984.

Truman, David B. The Governmental Process: Political Interests
and Public Opinion. New York, Alfred A. Knopf, 1962.

Verba, Sidney and Norman Nie. Participation in America. New
York, Harper and Row, 1972.

Wilson, James Q. Political Organizations. New York, Basic
Books, Inc., 1973.

Professional Journals

Arnstein, Sherry. "Maximum Feasible Manipulation." Public
Administration Review 32 (Sept., 1972), pp. 377-402.

Clark, Peter B. and James Q. Wilson. "Incentive Systems: A
Theory of Organizations." Administrative Science Quarterly
6 (1961), pp. 129-166.

Rich, Richard C. "A Political-Economy Approach to the Study of
Neighborhood Organizations." American Journal of Political
Science 4 (Nov. 1980), pp. 559-591.

Salisbury, Robert H. "An Exchange Theory of Interest Groups."
Midwest Journal of Political Science 13 (Feb., 1969), pp.
1-32.

Periodicals and Newspapers

Cloward, Richard A. and Frances Fox Piven. "Who Should be
Organized? 'Citizen Action' vs. 'Jobs and Justice'."
Working Papers for a New Society. May/June 1979, pp. 35-43.

Harrity, Mary Kay. "Putting Down Roots in Bridgeport."
Fairfield Advocate 2, No. 13 (14 Nov. 1979), pp. 6-7.

Kirby, Martin. "A Citizen Action Force that Really Works.
Southern Voices 10, No. 2 (May/June, 1974), n.p.

Kopkind, Andrew. "ACORN Calling: Door-to-Door Organizing in
Arkansas." Working Papers for a New Society 3, No. 3
(Summer, 1975), pp. 13-20.

Lovinger, Robert. "Can Harry Spence Fix Public Housing?" The
Boston Globe Magazine, 23 August 1981, p. 8.

149

POLITICAL ORGANIZING IN GRASSROOTS POLITICS

Norden, Eric. "Playboy Interview: Saul Alinsky." Playboy 9, No. 3, March, 1972, pp. 59-78 ff.

Walzer, Michael. "The Pastoral Retreat of the New Left." Dissent, Fall, 1979, pp. 4065 ff.

Pamphlets

"ACORN Community Organizing Model." Mimeographed, n.d.

"ACORN Members' Handbook." Mimeographed, n.d.

Community Organizing Handbook #2. New Orleans, The Institute for Social Justice, 2nd edition, 1979.

The People Decide. Program of the ACORN National Platform Conference, St. Louis, June 30-July 1, 1979.

Articles from Books

Kest, Steven and Wade Rathke. "ACORN: An Overview on its History, Structure, Methodology, Campaigns, and Philosophy as it Developed in Arkansas." Community Organizing Handbook #2. New Orleans, The Institute for Social Justice, 1979, pp. 3-13.

Silver, Mike. "Before and After the Action." Ed. Lee Staples. Westport, Connecticut, Greenwood Press, 1984.

Unpublished Dissertation

Delgado, Gary. "Organizing the Movement." Diss., University of California, Berkeley School of Social Work, 1984.

ACORN Members' Handbook, 39

ACORN organizers, 29; described, 42-43, 47, 52; experience of, 52-55; inspired by confrontation, 71; motives of 47-52; professional ethics of, 47, 79, 122-123; recruitment of, 49-50

ACORN Organizing Model, 34, 41-42, 43, 44, 57, 111; as source of political analysis, 113, 114-115, 118; organizational goals stated in, 30-31; promoting political participation, 122; sources of 30-31; terms of exchange in, 40

ACORN People's Platform, xi, 1, 36, 39, 117, 131-132

ACORN squatting campaign, 36, 72, 125, 127, 131

Adamson, Madeleine, 130-131

Alinsky, Saul, 14, 16, 30, 132-133; organizing strategy of, 24-25

Almond, Gabriel and Sidney Verba, 15

Anger, used in organizing; by ACORN, 55, 57-58, 59, 62, 114-115; by Alinsky, 17

Anti-corporatism, 35, 36-37, 38, 39, 124, 130, 132

Anti-intellectualism, 35, 37

Arnstein, Sherry, 16

Bailis, Lawrence, 22

Barnard, Chester, 3

Boston Model (of NWRO), 30

Borgos, Seth, 130-131